Mathew Cerletty

Drawings

Karma

Naomi
Fry

It Costs a Lot of Money to Look This Cheap

It was June 2021, and Kanye West was looking ahead. The previous summer, the rapper and designer had signed a ten-year contract with the Gap to create a version of his own Yeezy clothing line for the retailer; now, he was revealing for the first time an item from the new partnership. That item—a blue puffer jacket—was, in itself, quite plain. And yet there was something striking, indeed almost mesmerizing, about the way it was presented. There it was, on Instagram, on the Gap's website, and even figured in outsized, spectral projections on buildings in New York, Los Angeles, and Chicago: a bright cobalt nylon thing, shiny, with a rounded drop shoulder that, crucially, was shown not on the figure of a model, but rather on its own—an object qua object.

Looking at the jacket, I was reminded, perhaps a bit strangely, of the tapir bone tossed by the man-ape at the beginning of Stanley Kubrick's *2001: A Space Odyssey*. A common tool, initially prized for its use value (earlier in the scene, it is employed as a bludgeon with which to bash the animal skeleton it had once been a part of), the bone becomes a talisman as it spins through the air. Featured in its various virtual formats, West's jacket seemed to take on a similar resonance. Floating ambiently, it was itself a kind of talisman, appearing to hold within its silent folds the mysteries of the universe. Looking at it, I felt as if it was on the verge of speaking. What would it say if it did? And yet, this odd, inexplicable magic was coupled with utter banality. The jacket was, after all, just a piece of apparel, made of humble synthetics, ultimately destined for nothing more than the quotidian indignities the world would surely meet it with—the wear and tear of coffee spills and mud splatters, of rain and sleet and snow.

A similar tension animates the work of Mathew Cerletty, who, in his paintings and drawings, captures a variety of objects in the world in both their magic and mundanity. In the course of the past decade and a half, Cerletty has occupied himself with building, through meticulous representation, an empire of things. Sometimes, the situations he paints are heightened and surreal, nearly Magritte-esque in the blunt, graphic simplicity their odd juxtapositions offer: a wood plank floor leading to a white door that, prop-like, opens not to a room, but to a lush lawn, so green it's nearly turquoise, and to a vast, velvety night sky beyond it; or a blocky copy of the Yellow Pages, as hard-edged and uniform as a painted canvas, floating, inexplicably, on open waters. Other times, the objects Cerletty figures appear wholly unremarkable, as if plucked straight from daily life: a man's brown leather belt, looped over itself; a couple of manila envelopes, side by side; a plush, long-eared stuffed-toy bunny.

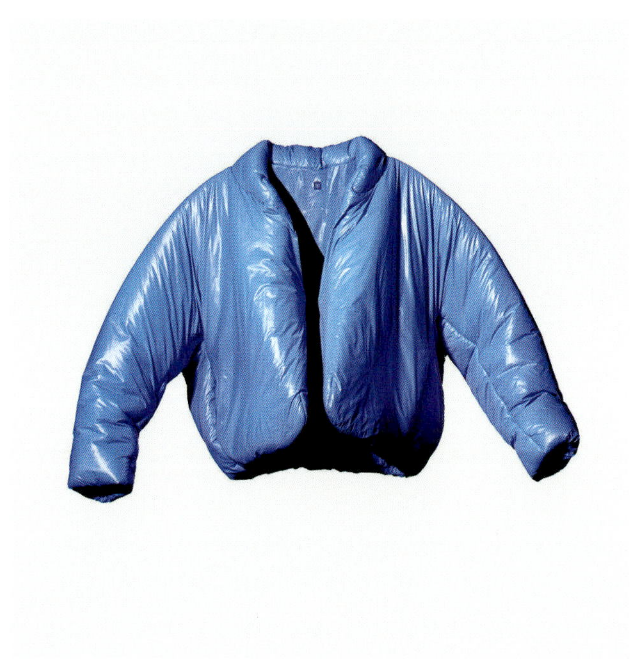

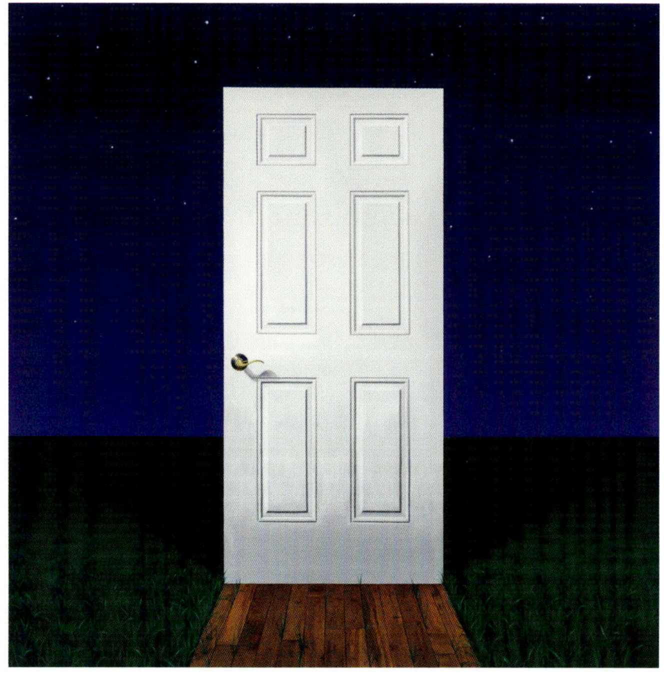

The multivalence of Cerletty's objects—their banality as well as their mystery—is in some ways like that of Marx's commodities. ("A commodity appears, at first sight, a very trivial thing," Marx famously wrote, in the first chapter of *Capital*. "Its analysis shows that it is, in fact, a very queer thing.") And yet, the things Cerletty paints are almost too anonymous, too aggressively bland, to be called commodities. Certainly, they don't inspire the fetishistic lust that we would associate with that which is aroused by the prized fruit of capitalistic production. Looking at the paintings, I sometimes wondered: *what reason did the artist have to expend so much labor on representing* these *things, in particular?* In this way, Cerletty's work is not unlike the high-touch photographs of Gregory Crewdson and Thomas Demand, in which built environments are meticulously recreated as *sets* (in Crewdson's case, peopled and human-scale; in Demand's case, modeled out of paper and deserted) and captured by the camera. We are aware of the work that it took to create the scenes on view—as routine as they might appear at first glance—and that knowledge turns them eerie and thick with implied meaning. Cerletty's drawings and paintings, too, awaken not a covetousness, but a kind of fear. The door he chooses to paint is the most usual and prefab Home Depot-style door one could find, but it is also a portal to nothingness: cross its threshold, and you might fall off the edge of the earth. The brown belt, floating in space like the door—or, indeed, like West's jacket—is coiled, snake-like, as if ready to spring into action at any moment. It might be pulled through the loops of a pair of chinos, or it might just as easily be thrown over a curtain rod or a lamp and tightened into a noose, to slip around one's neck. To look at Cerletty's work is, in this sense, to feel the controlled tension of a horror movie.

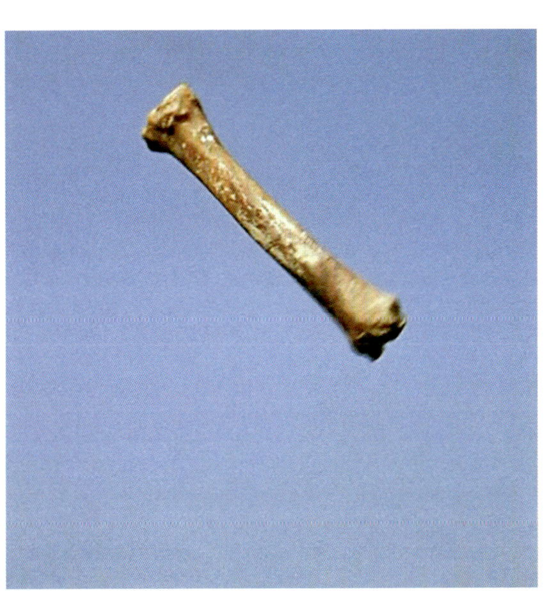

But there is something not just scary but also a little bit funny about all this. To spend weeks and months creating a gorgeously meticulous rendering of a bulbous head of broccoli, or a wooden laundry-drying rack—what a ridiculous endeavor that is! Almost as ridiculous as projecting a larger-than-life blue jacket on the side of a building, though Cerletty, perhaps unlike West, is in on the joke. And this might be especially true, I think, in his drawings, nine of which are presented in this show. Unlike the artist's paintings, which are seamless and nearly scientific in their hyper-realism, his drawings are warmer, and more clearly reflect the labor exerted by the human hand. A yellow rubber duckie on a white background; a brown bag of groceries, among them a bunch of bananas and some leafy greens, floating in a beige expanse; a pair of purple dishwashing gloves, their fingers turned up beseechingly against a lavender backdrop; a terracotta planter; a plush green ottoman: in all of these drawings, we can see the repetitive, graduated strokes of Cerletty's colored pencils, the illusion of an airtight surface falling just a step short from convincing the viewer. The relative obviousness of the ruse ups the ante: *Here, I am showing you my work*, Cerletty seems to say. *Isn't it funny what I did to get here? Isn't it, too, a little weird? Maybe, also, a little scary?*

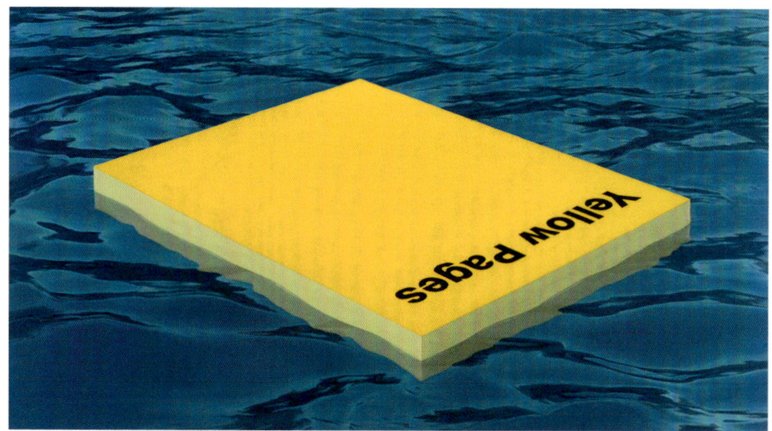

Looking at these drawings, I found myself thinking suddenly of a well-known Dolly Parton quote: "It costs a lot of money to look this cheap." Parton's well-earned icon status has relied not only on her great talents as a performer and musician, but also on a kind of platinum-bouffanted, painted and tartish femininity, and her admission of the effort that goes into the seemingly "cheap," effortless surface of her appearance is not just funny, but frank, too. There is something almost Marxian about this attitude: *let me show you the labor that goes into the product that is me*, she is saying. *Let me show you what it takes to be an object, and in the process, reveal myself as a subject.* An object speaking, saying things, telling us its secrets, revealing its subject-like qualities—that is a rare thing, a gift, and this is something that Cerletty's work generously offers us. His drawings center the objects he chooses to represent, show them close-up, on their own, the hand imbuing them with meaning. They become, in this way, portraits. They are, in their fullness, just like people: plain and odd and funny and boring and terrifying. We look at them, and ask ourselves what they will do next.

Images: The Yeezy Gap Jacket; Mathew Cerletty, *Night Door*, 2013; Still from Stanley Kubrick's *2001: A Space Odyssey*, 1968, (detail); Mathew Cerletty, *Yellow Pages*, 2015; Mathew Cerletty, *The Belt*, 2020; Dolly Parton

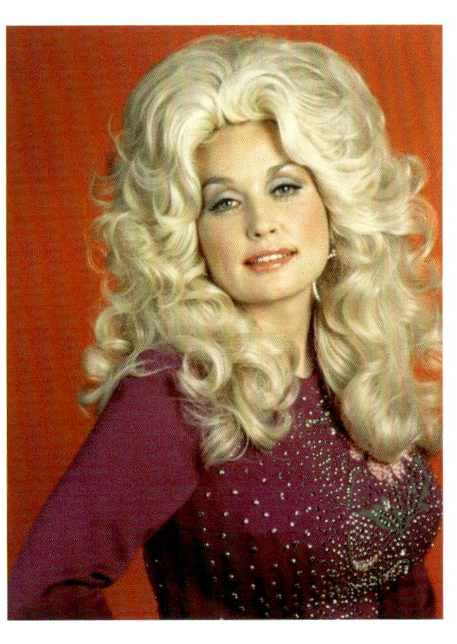

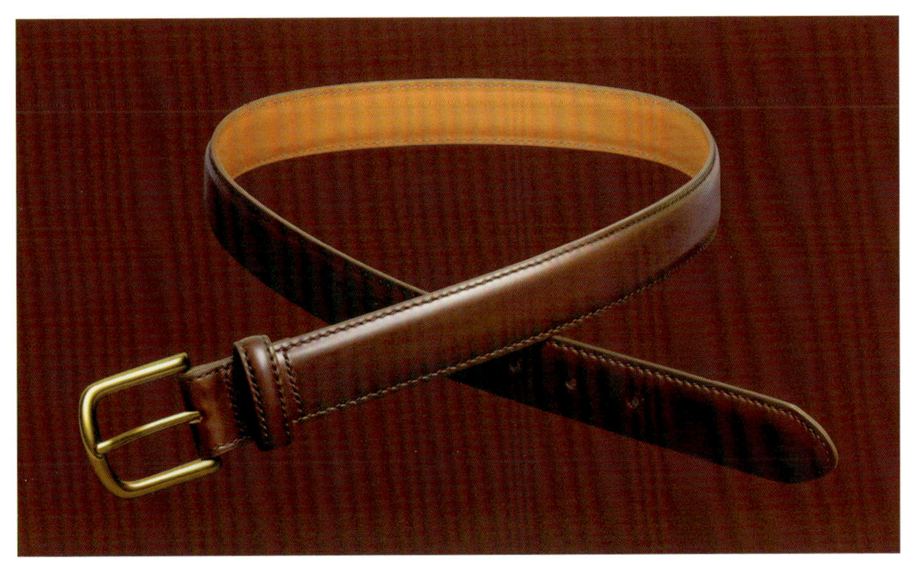

Help, 2021
Colored pencil on paper
26¾ × 24 inches

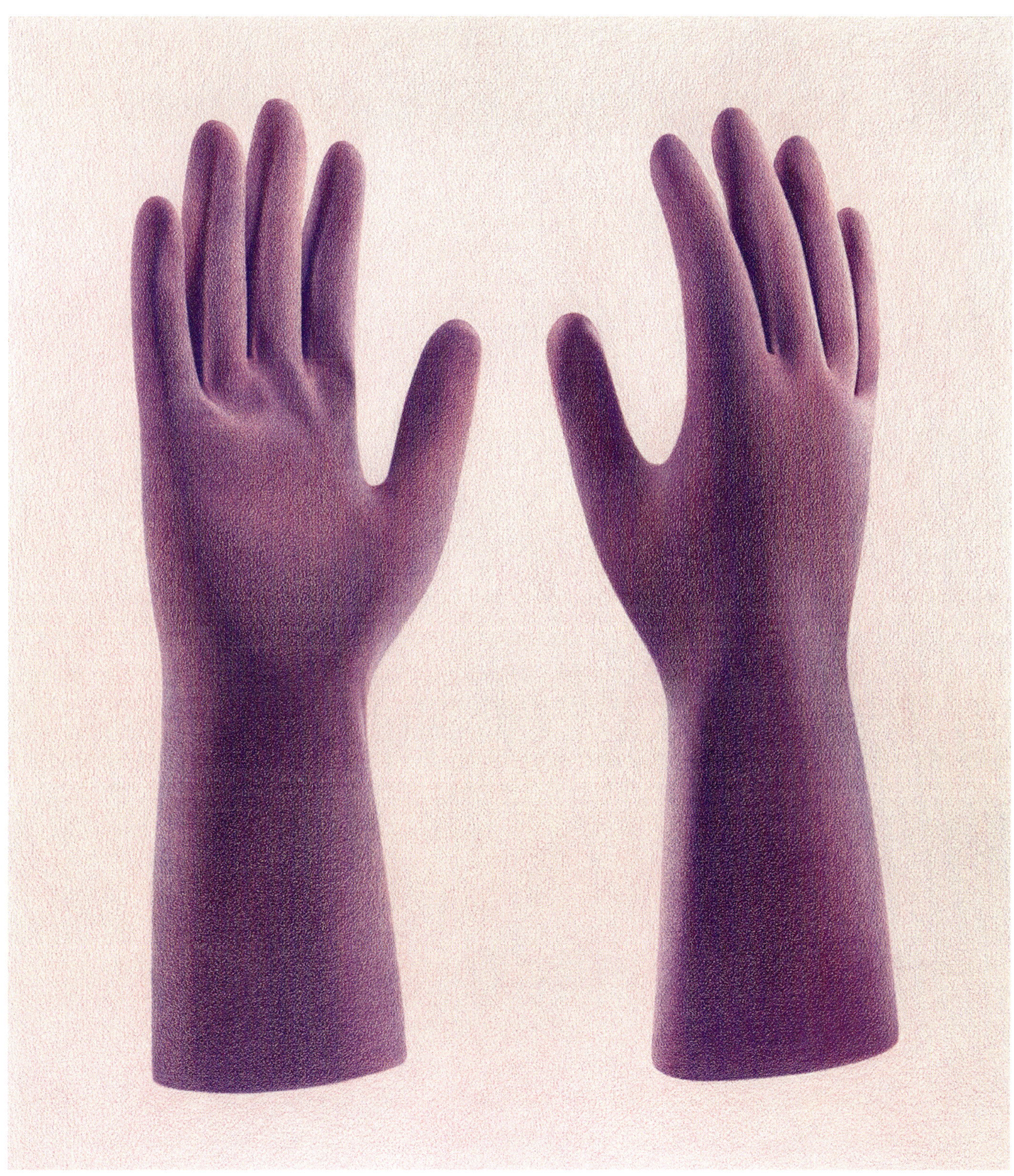

Golden Girl, 2021
Colored pencil on paper
23 × 30 inches

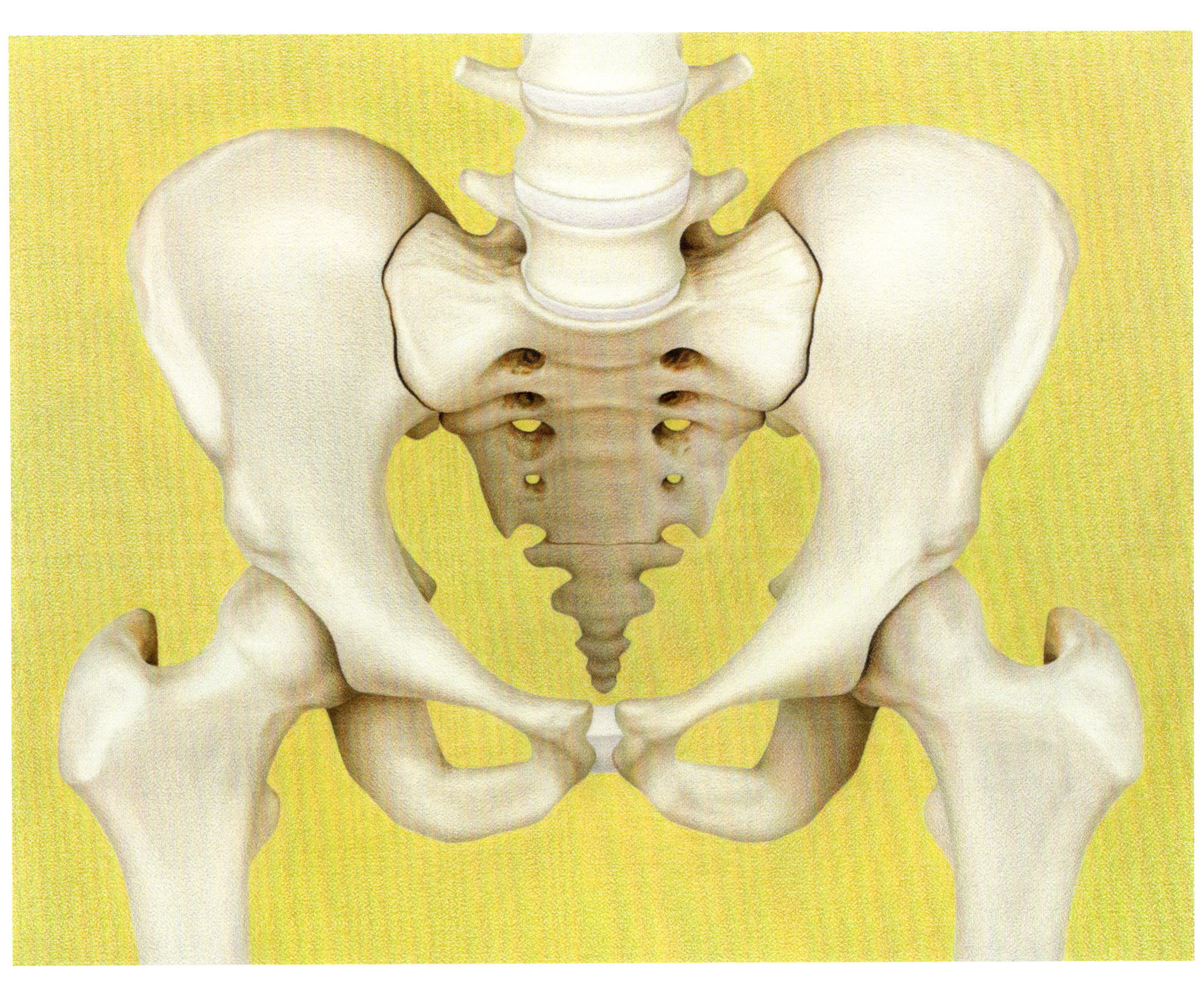

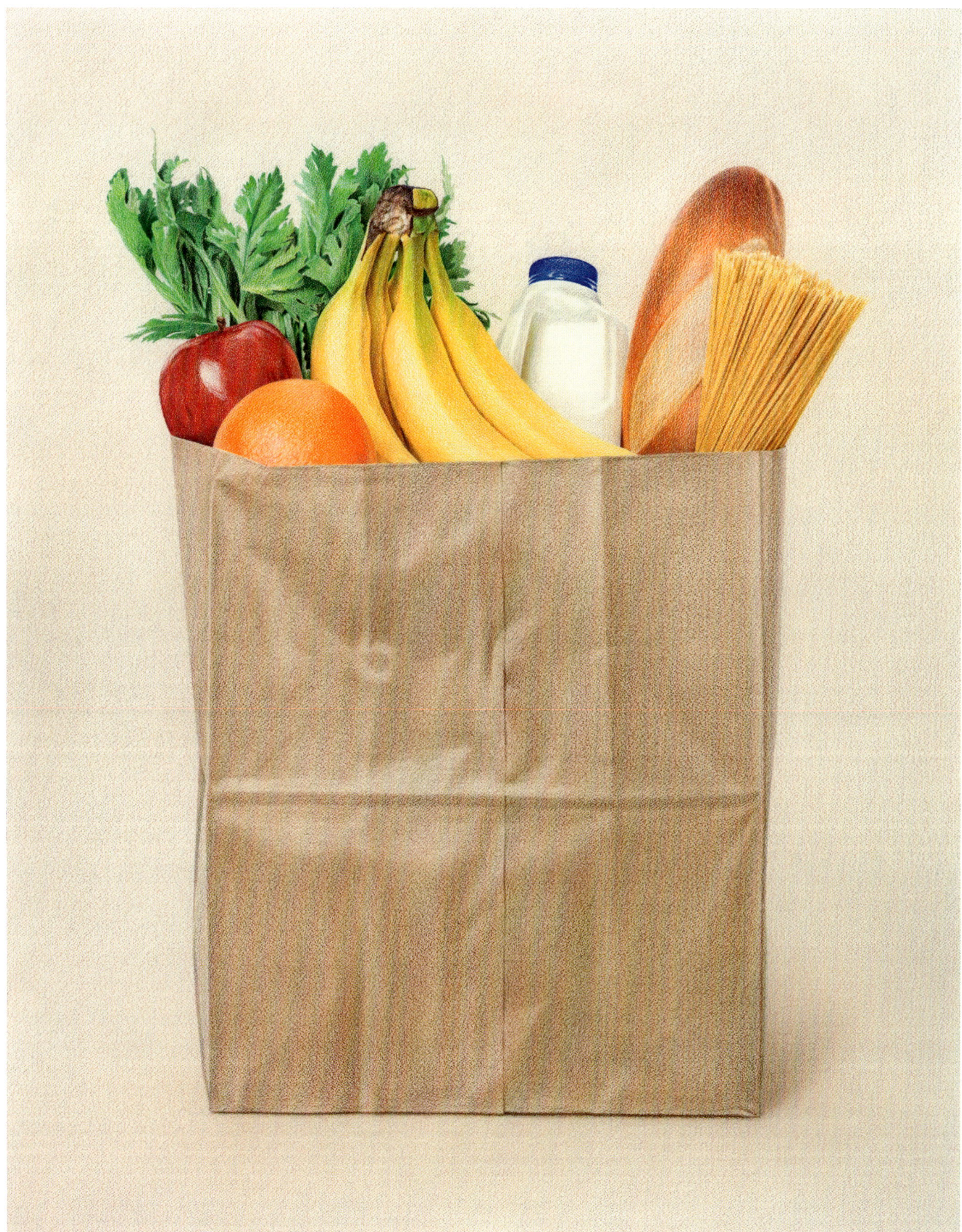

Groceries, 2021
Colored pencil on paper
31¼ × 25 inches

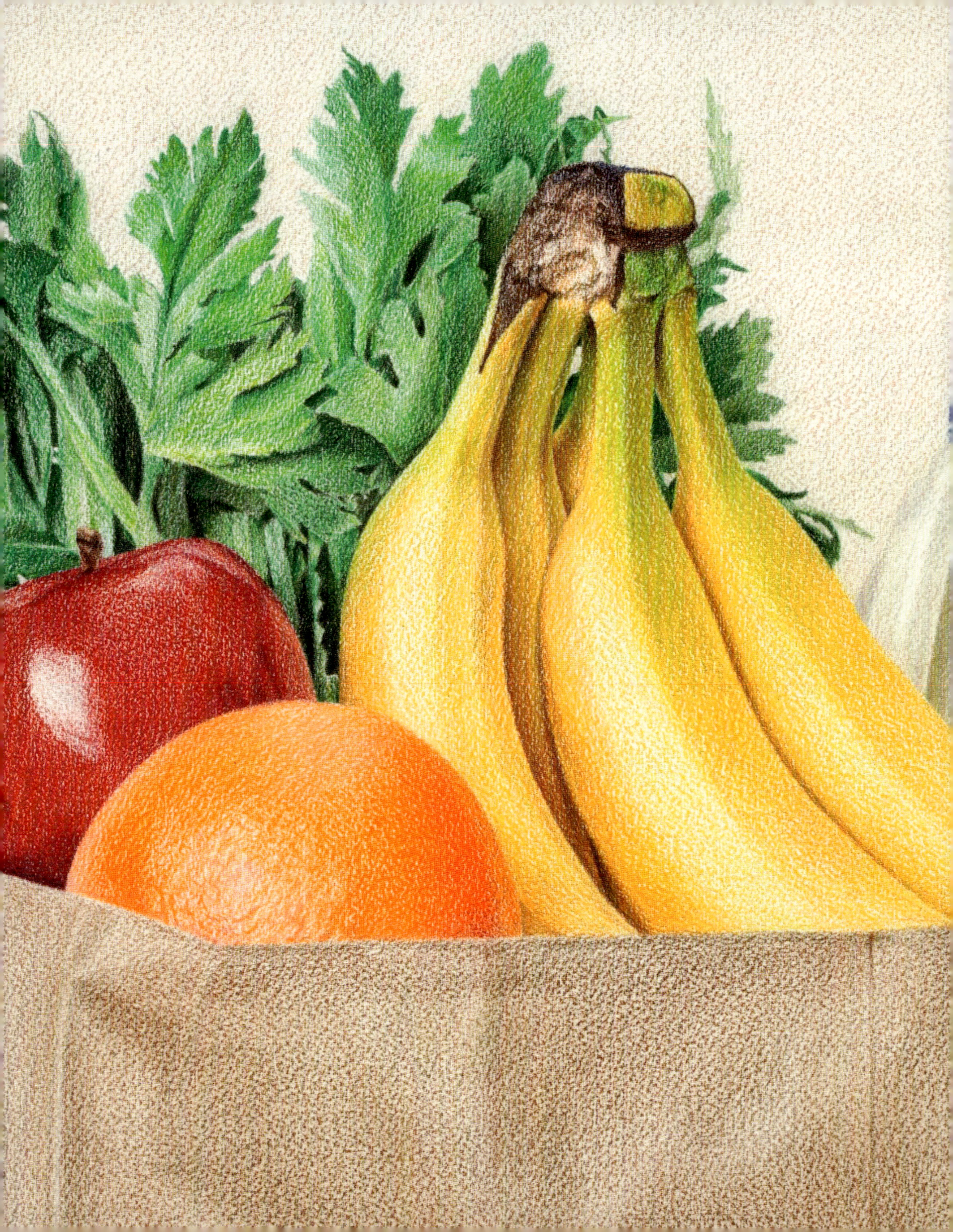

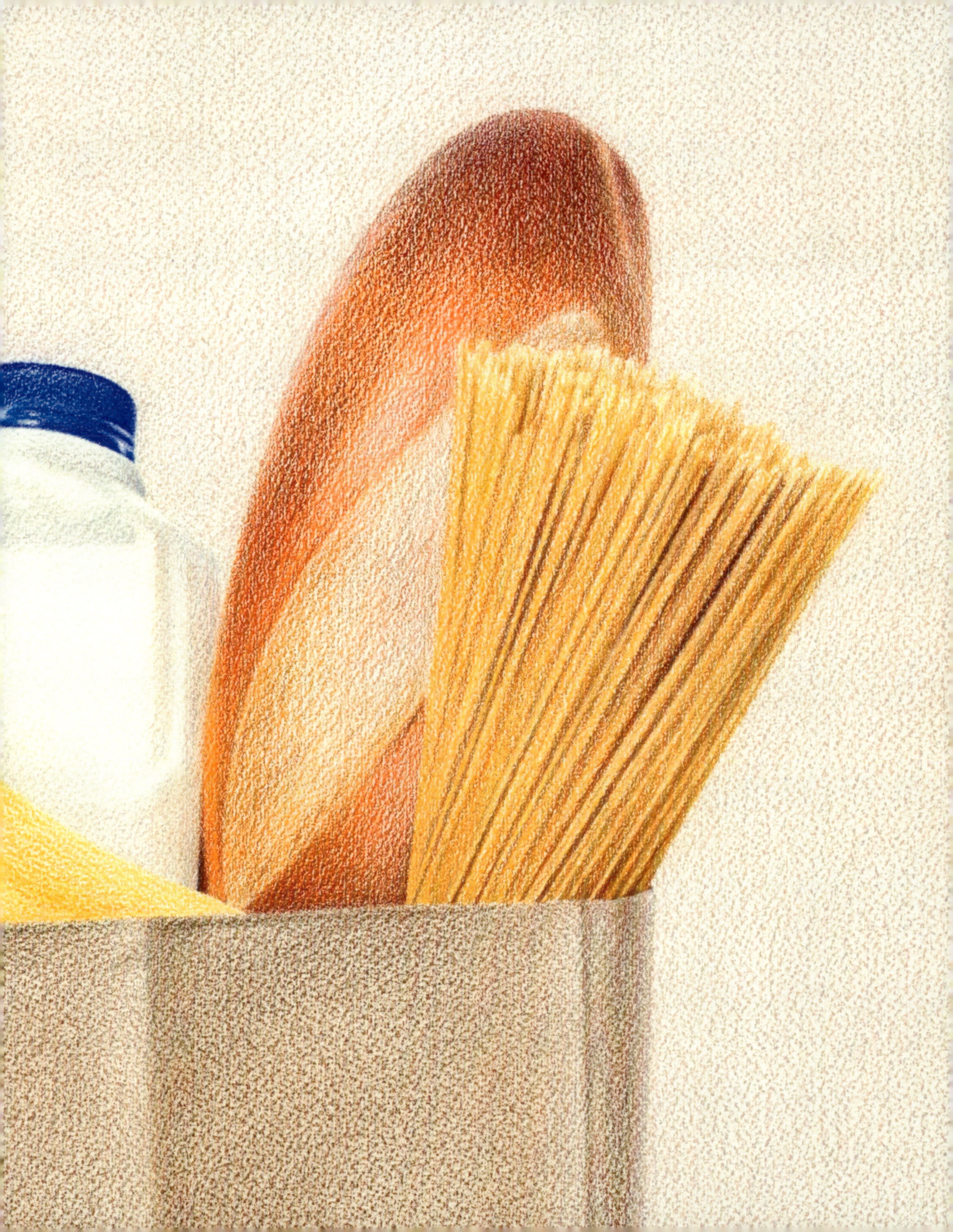

You're the One, 2020
Colored pencil on paper
25 × 20¼ inches

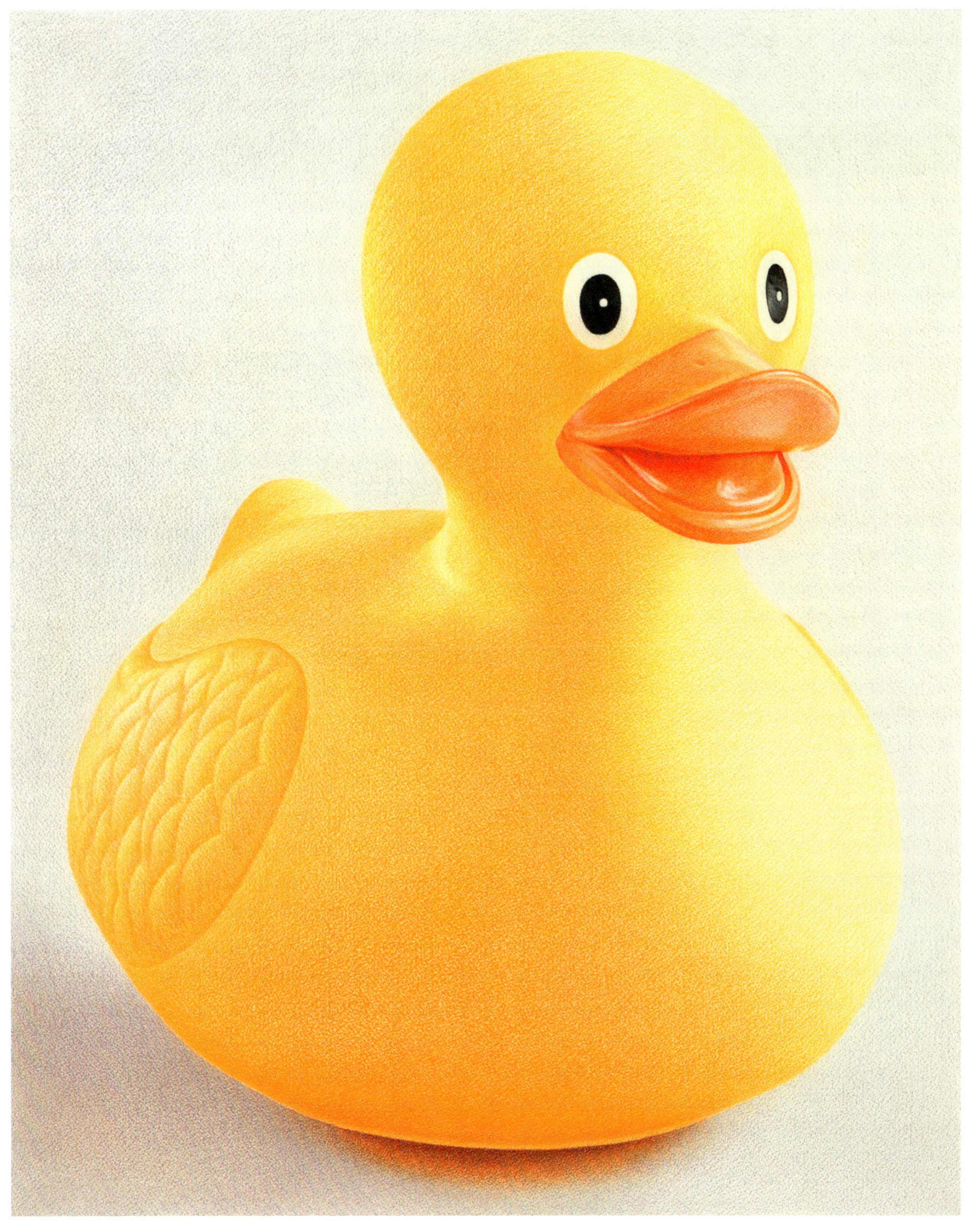

Back to Basics, 2018
Colored pencil on paper
30 × 36 inches

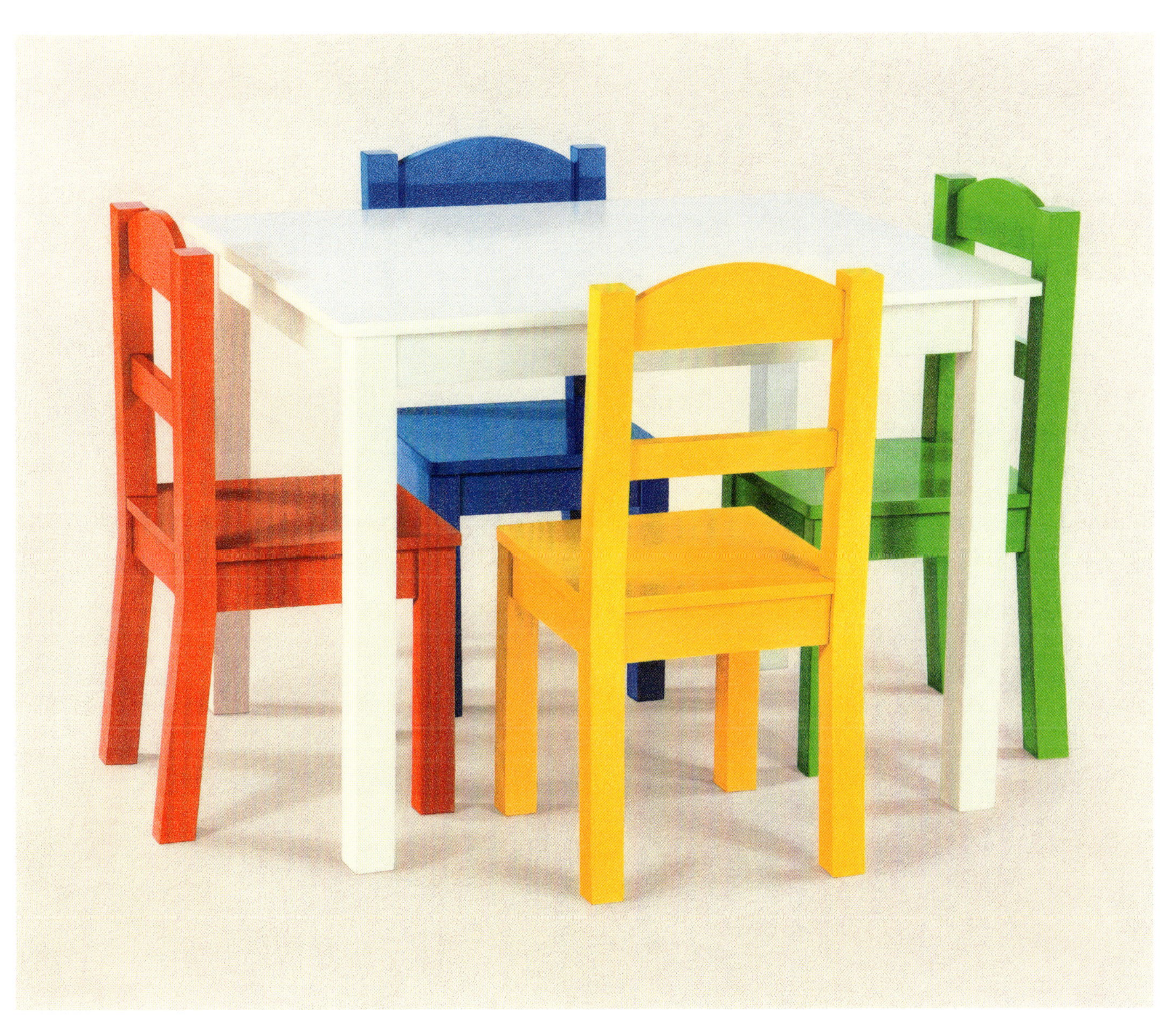

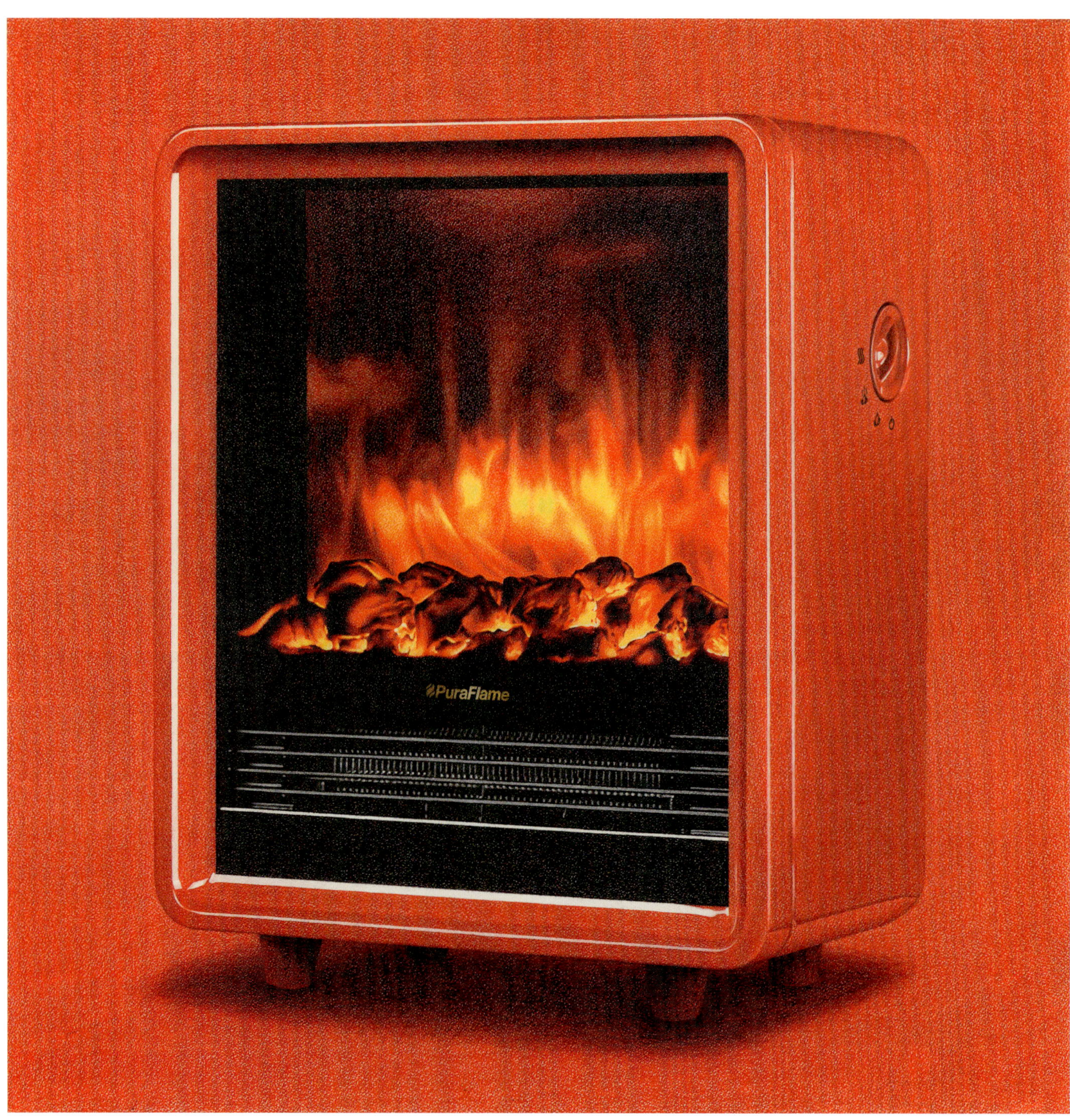
PuraFlame

PuraFlame, 2018
Colored pencil on paper
25 × 25 inches

Centerpiece, 2018
Colored pencil on paper
23¾ × 20 inches

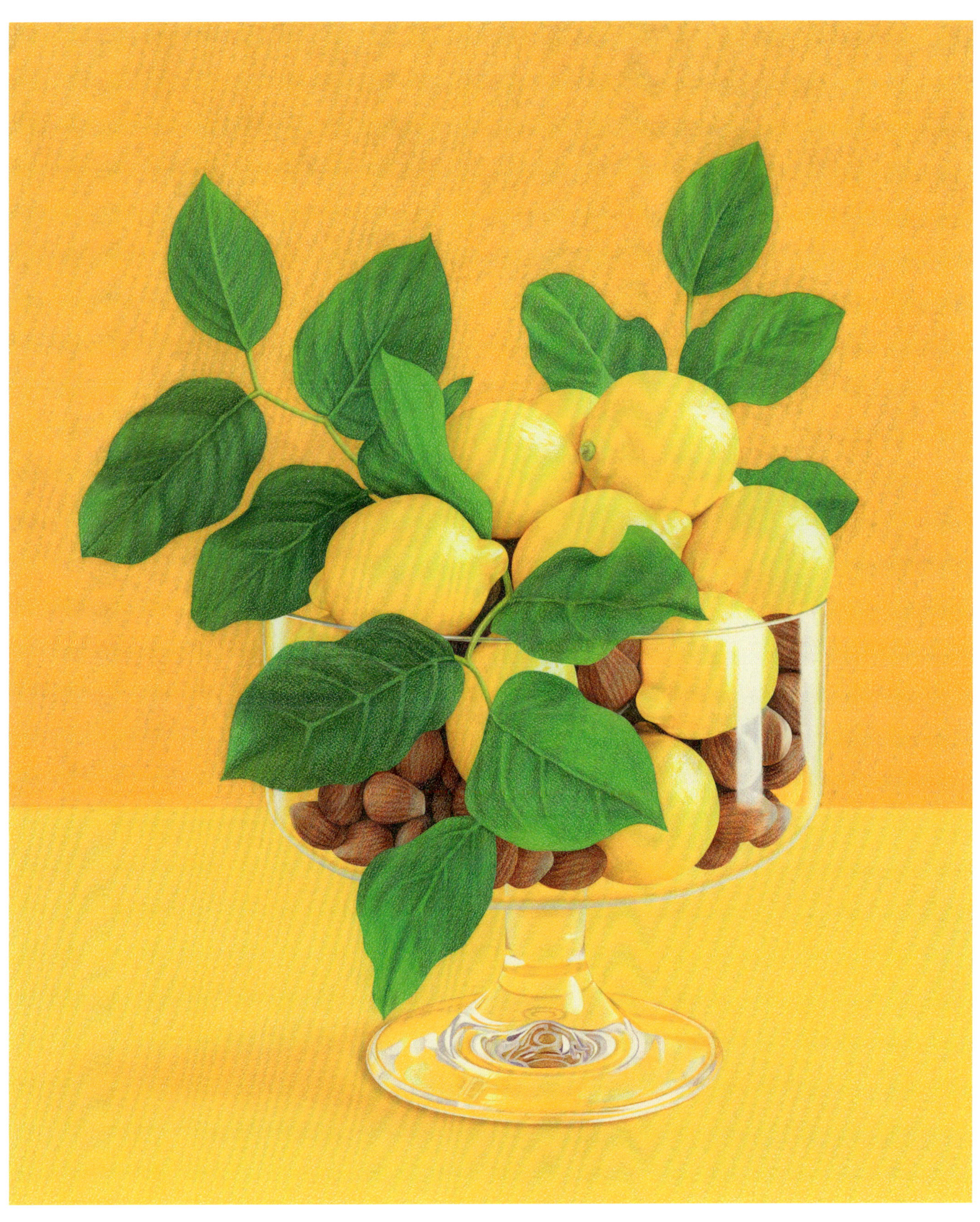

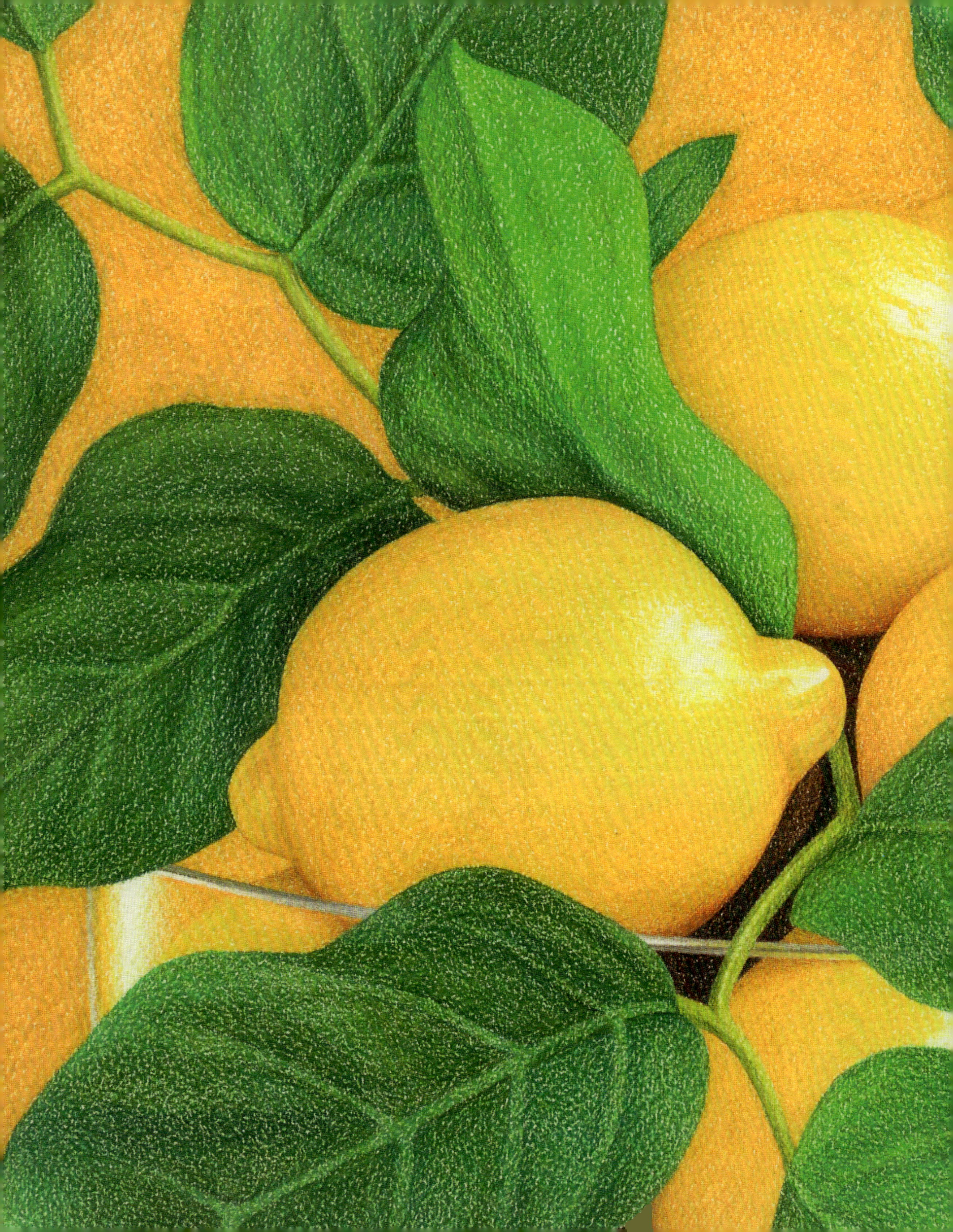

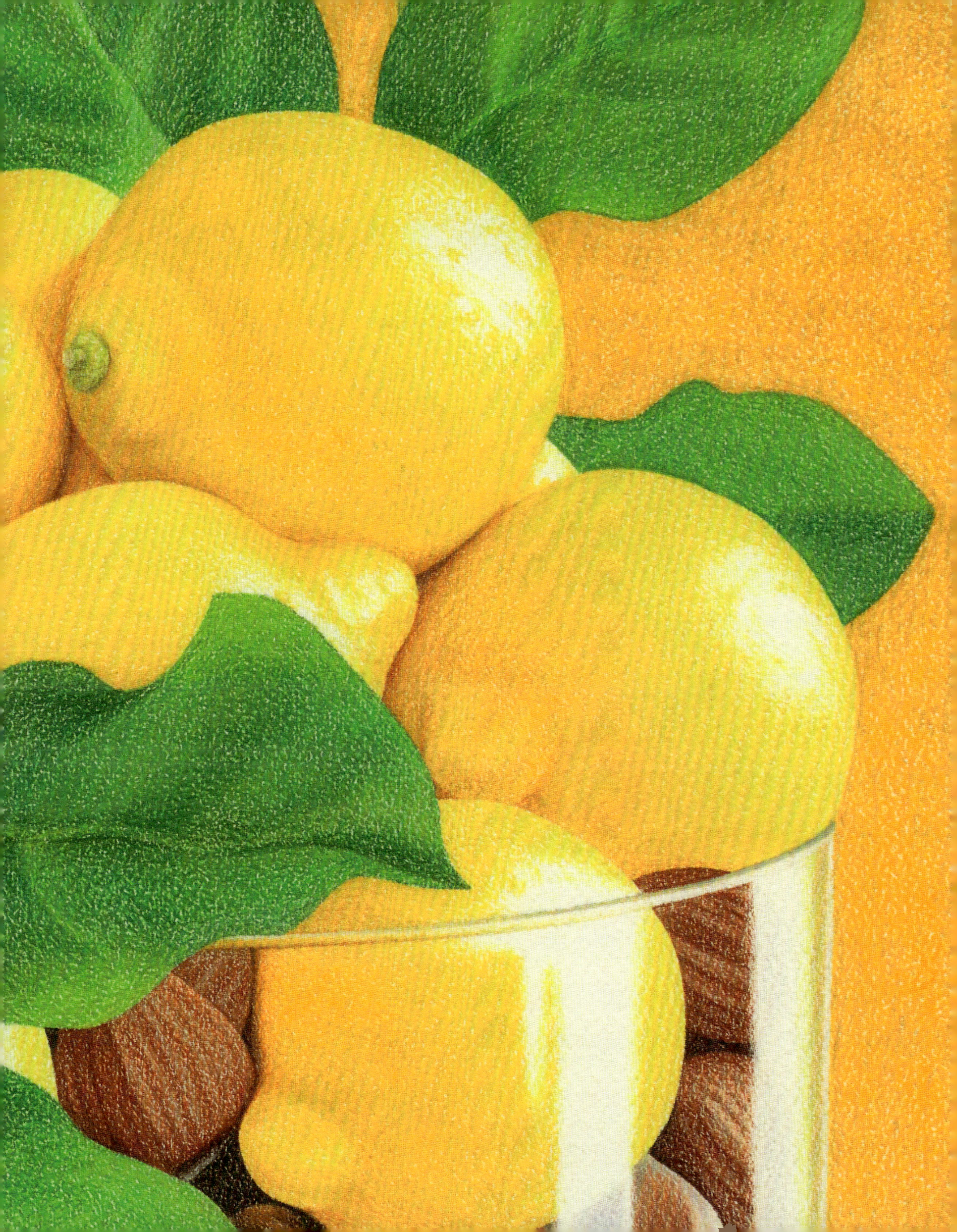

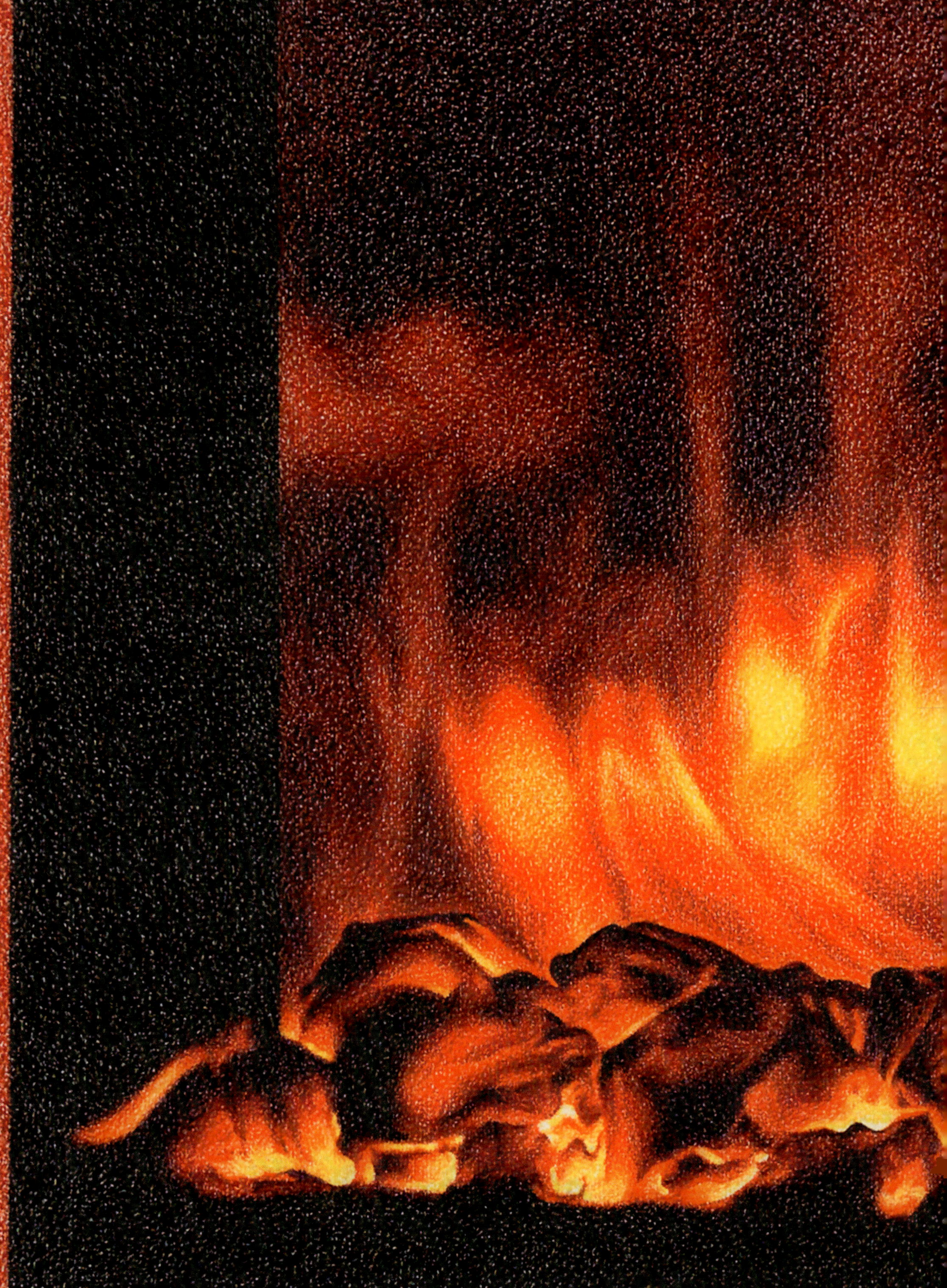
PuraFlame

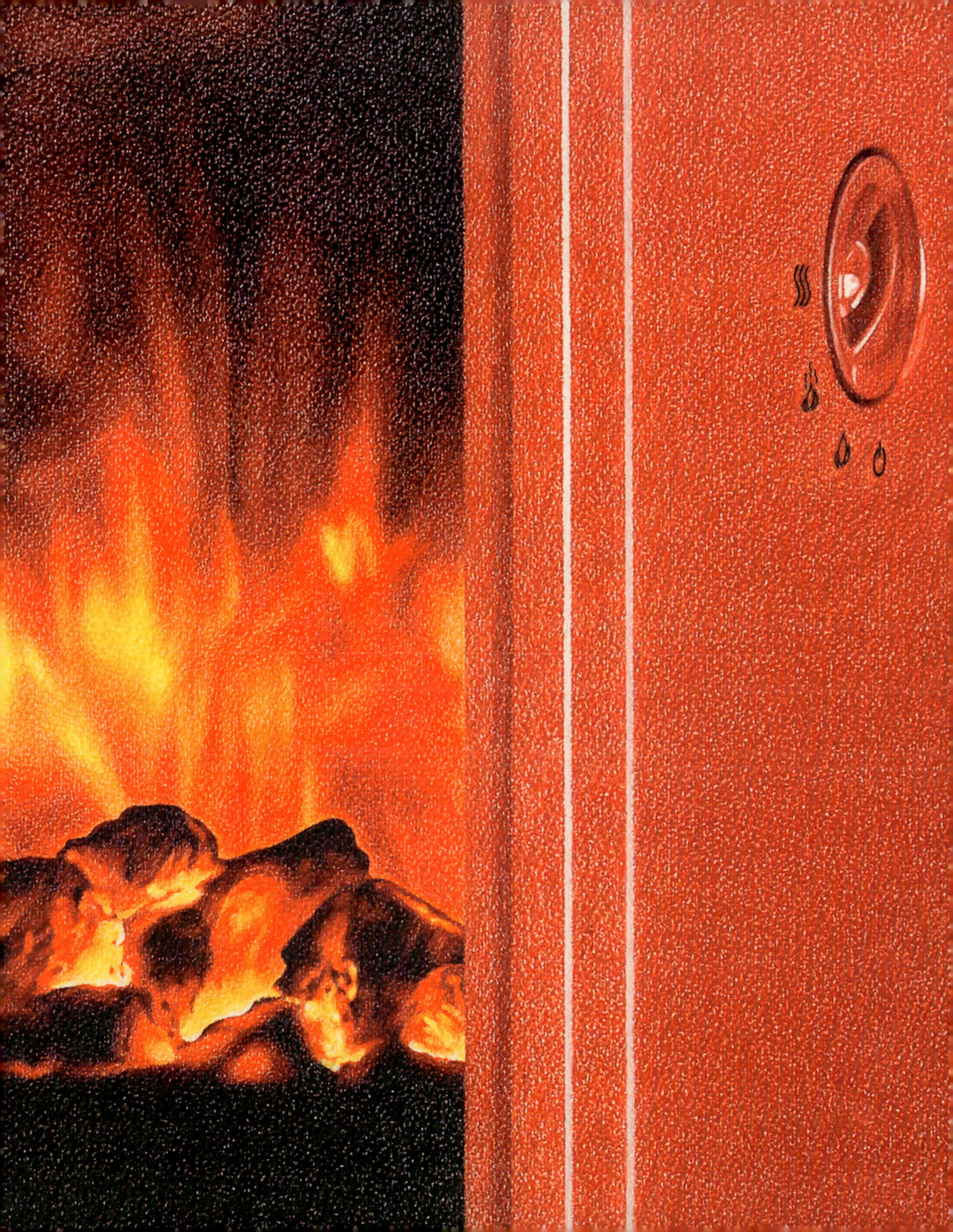

Far Out, 2020
Colored pencil on paper
21½ × 17¼ inches

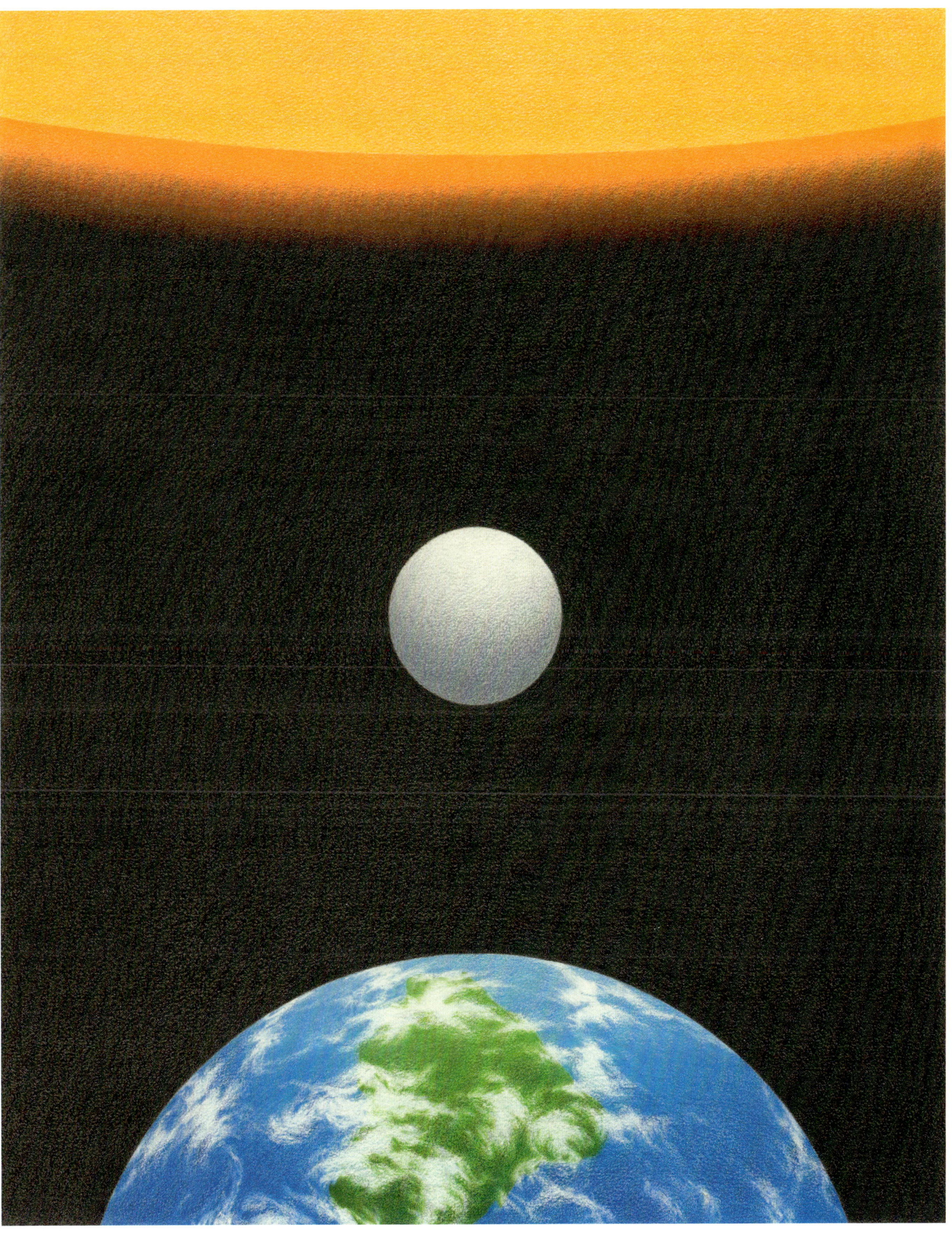

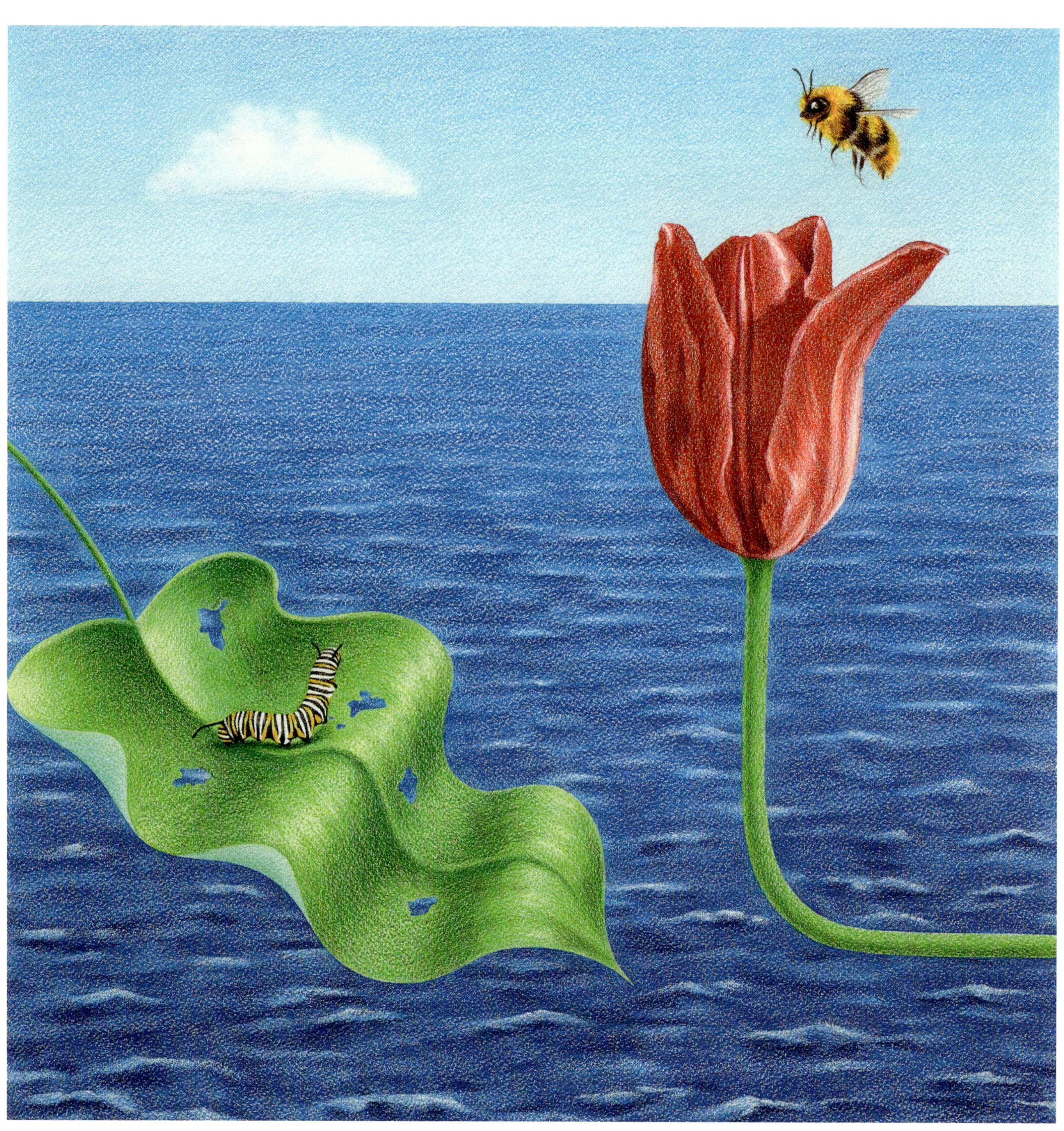

Old California, 2017
Colored pencil on paper
15¼ × 15 inches

Heart, 2021
Colored pencil on paper
20¼ × 14½ inches

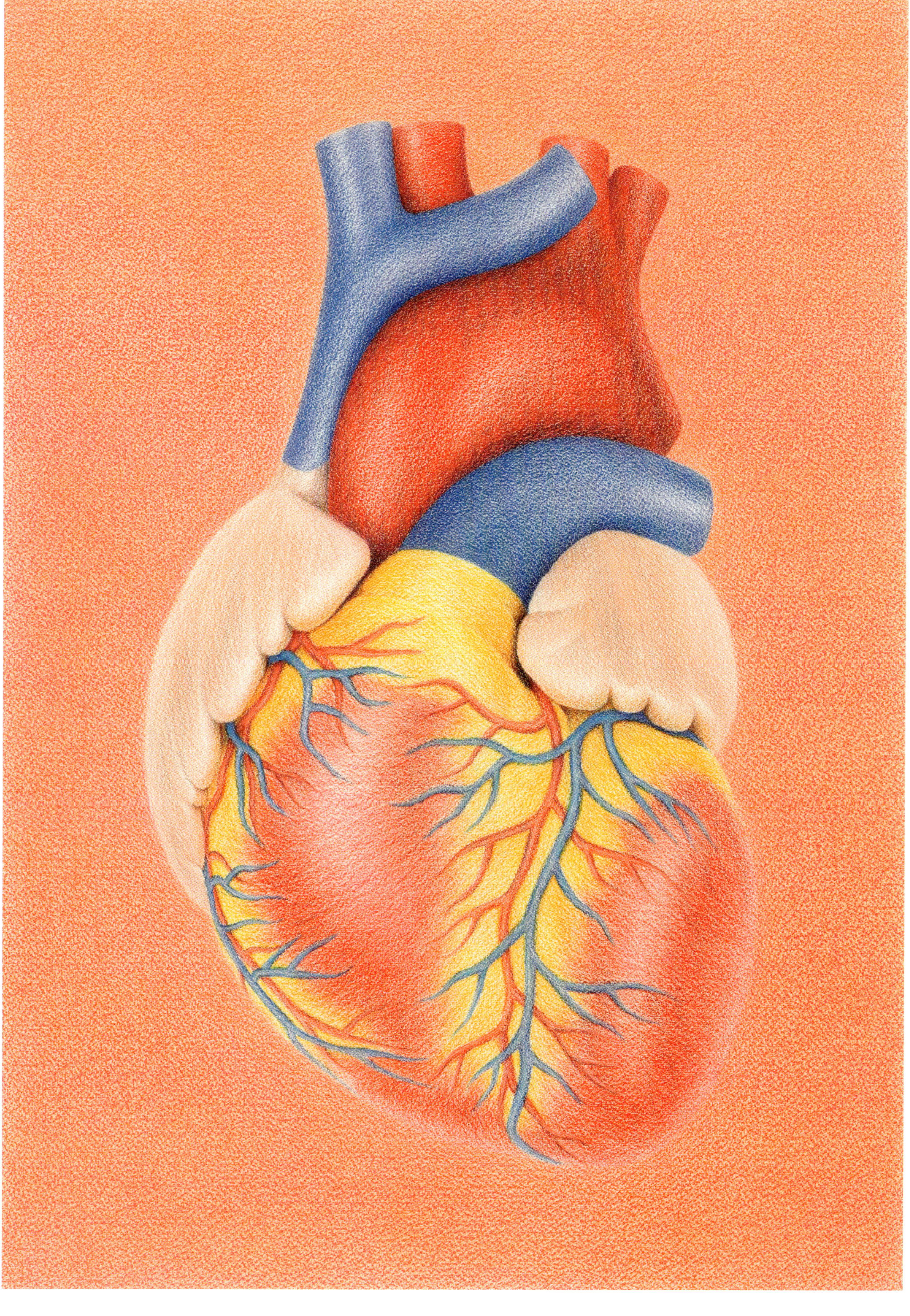

Friends, 2017
Colored pencil on paper
26¼ × 20¾ inches

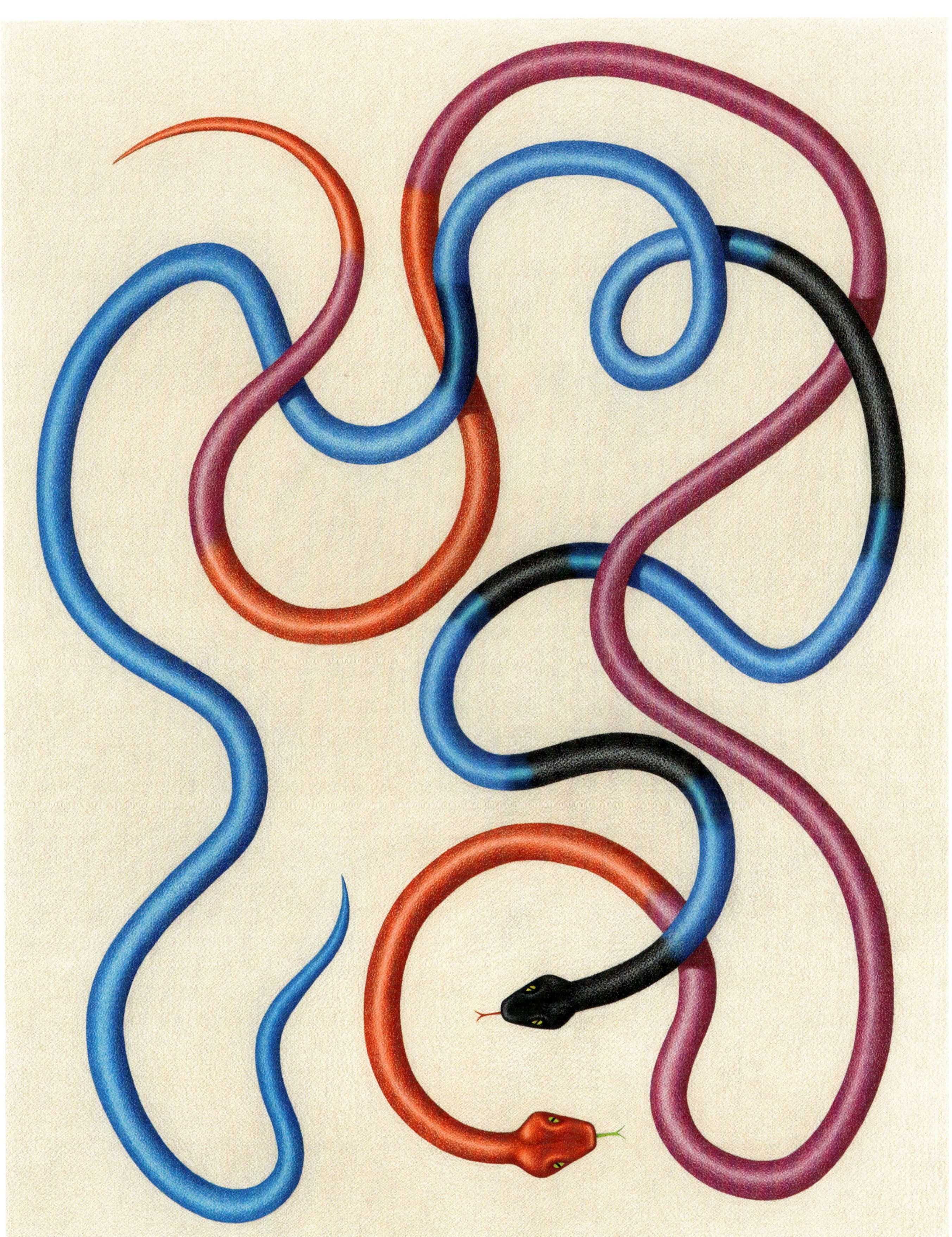

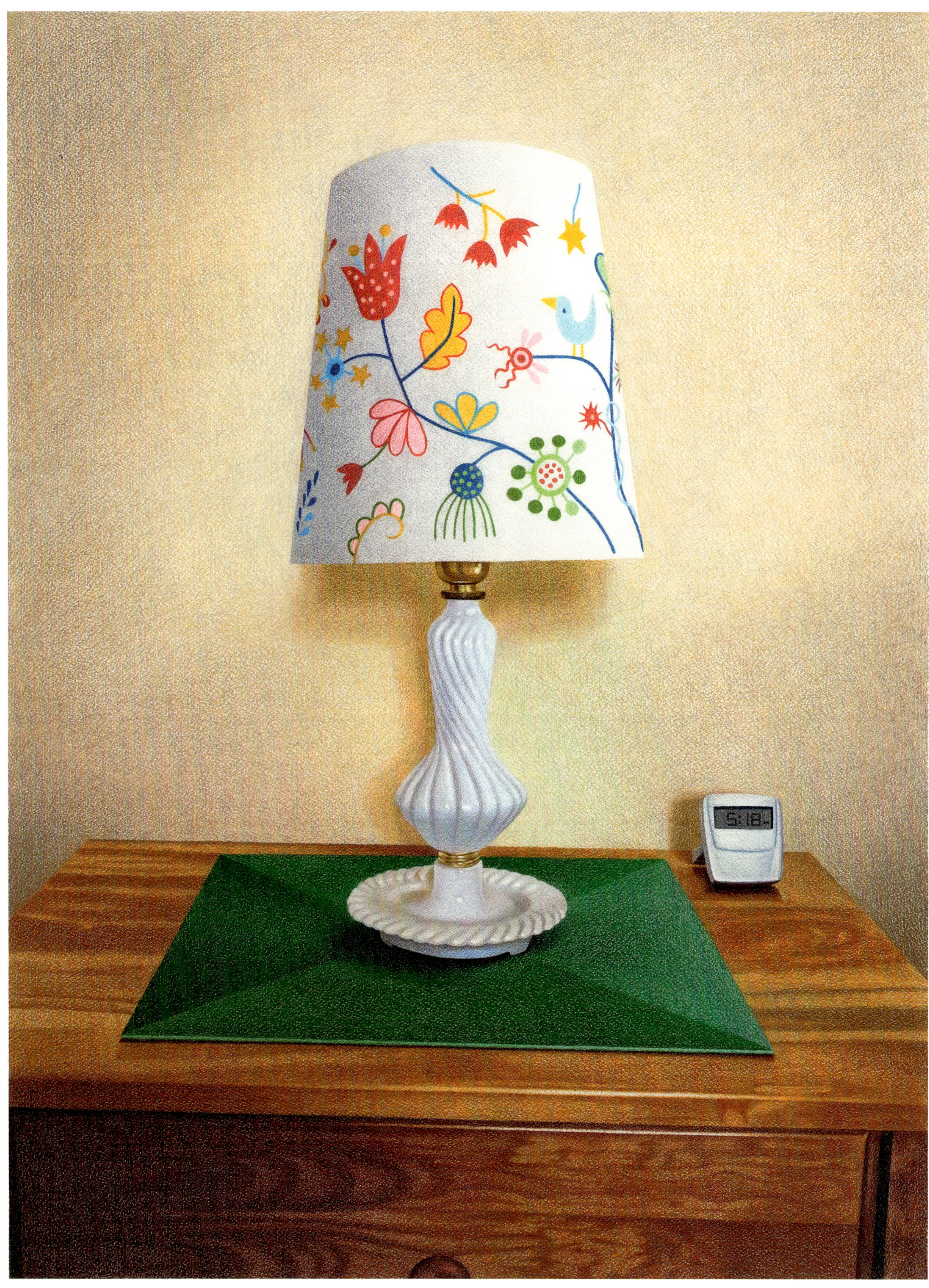
5:18

Mitchell's Lamp, 2017
Colored pencil on paper
25 × 18¾ inches

Shelf Life, 2017
Colored pencil on paper
31¾ × 38 inches

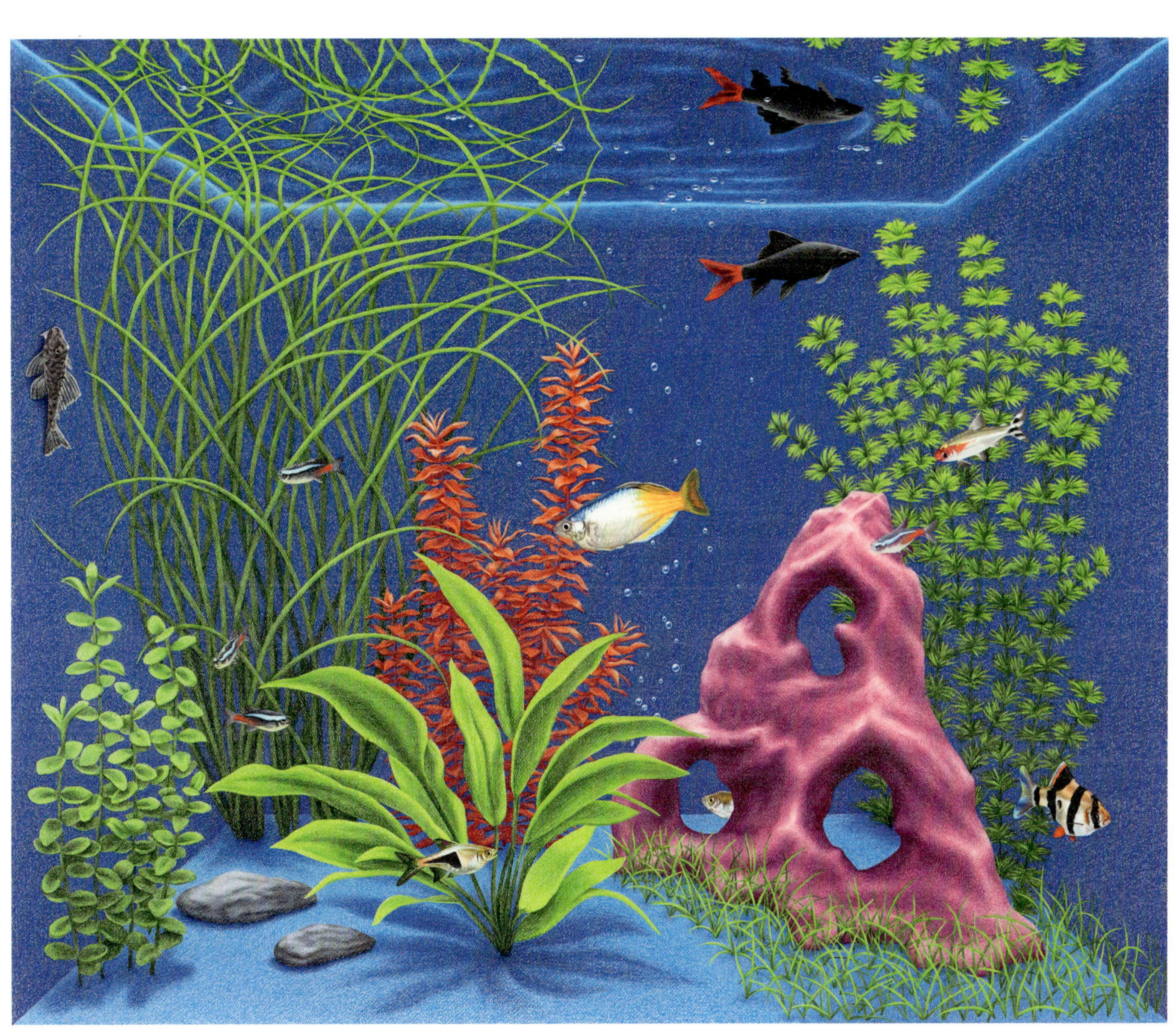

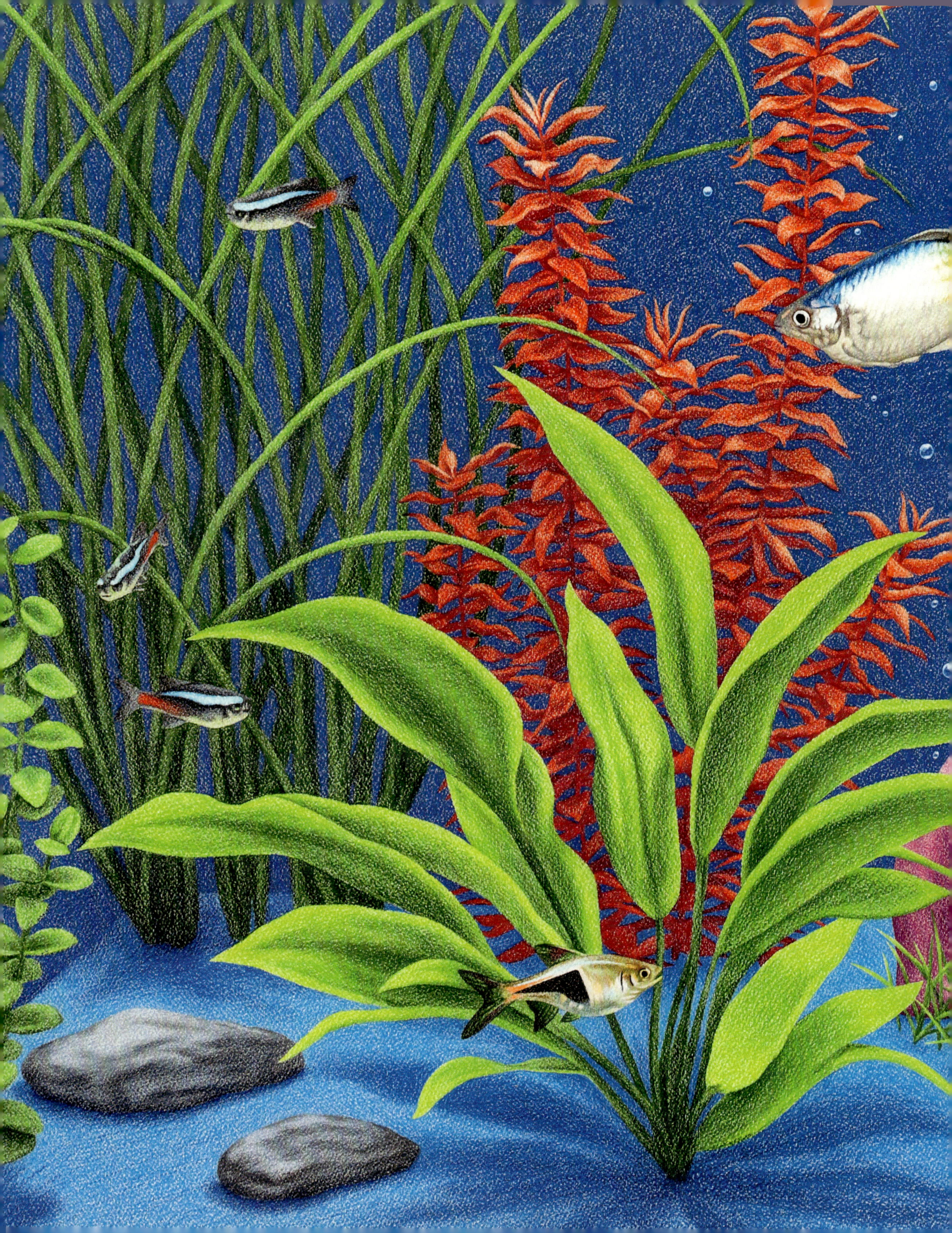

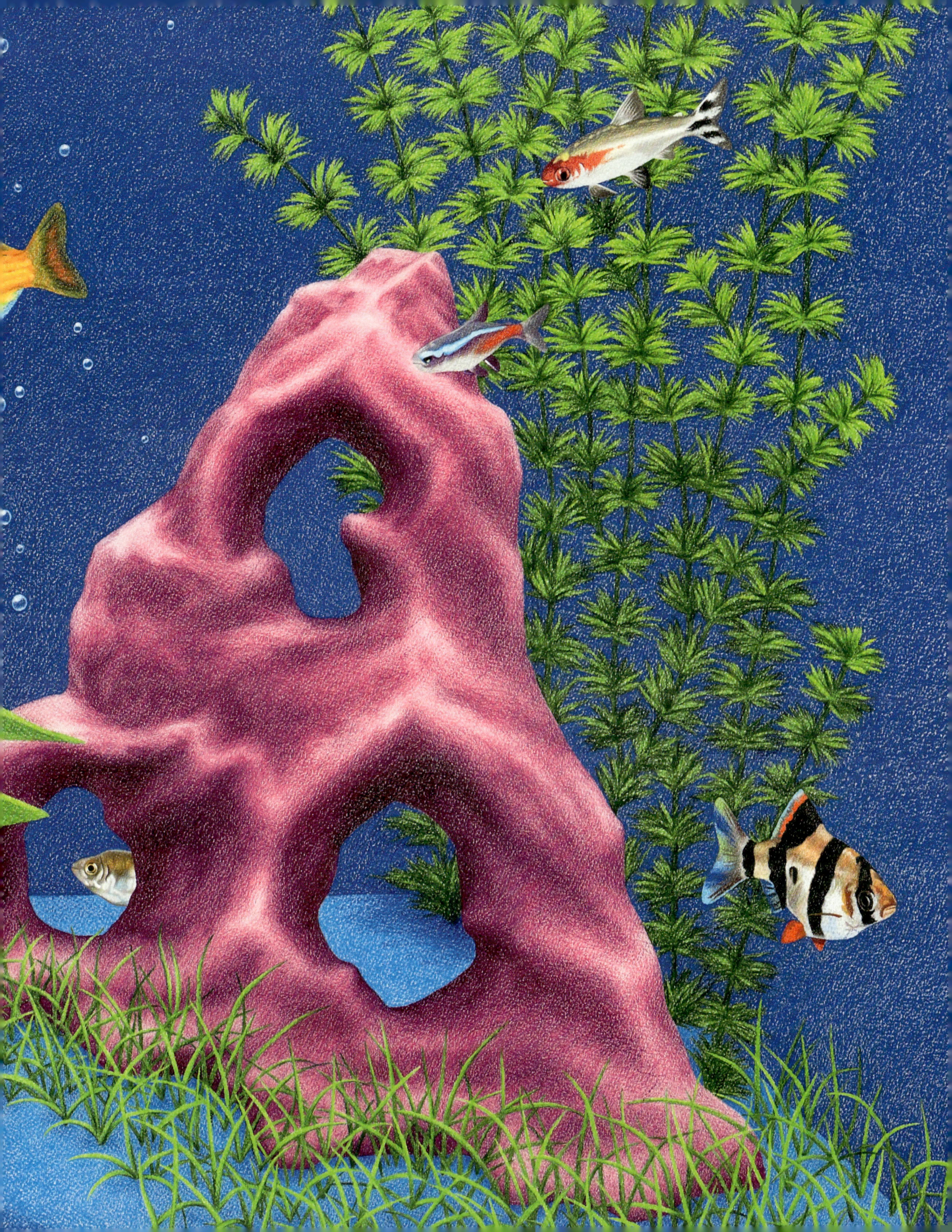

This, 2016
Colored pencil on paper
21 × 25½ inches

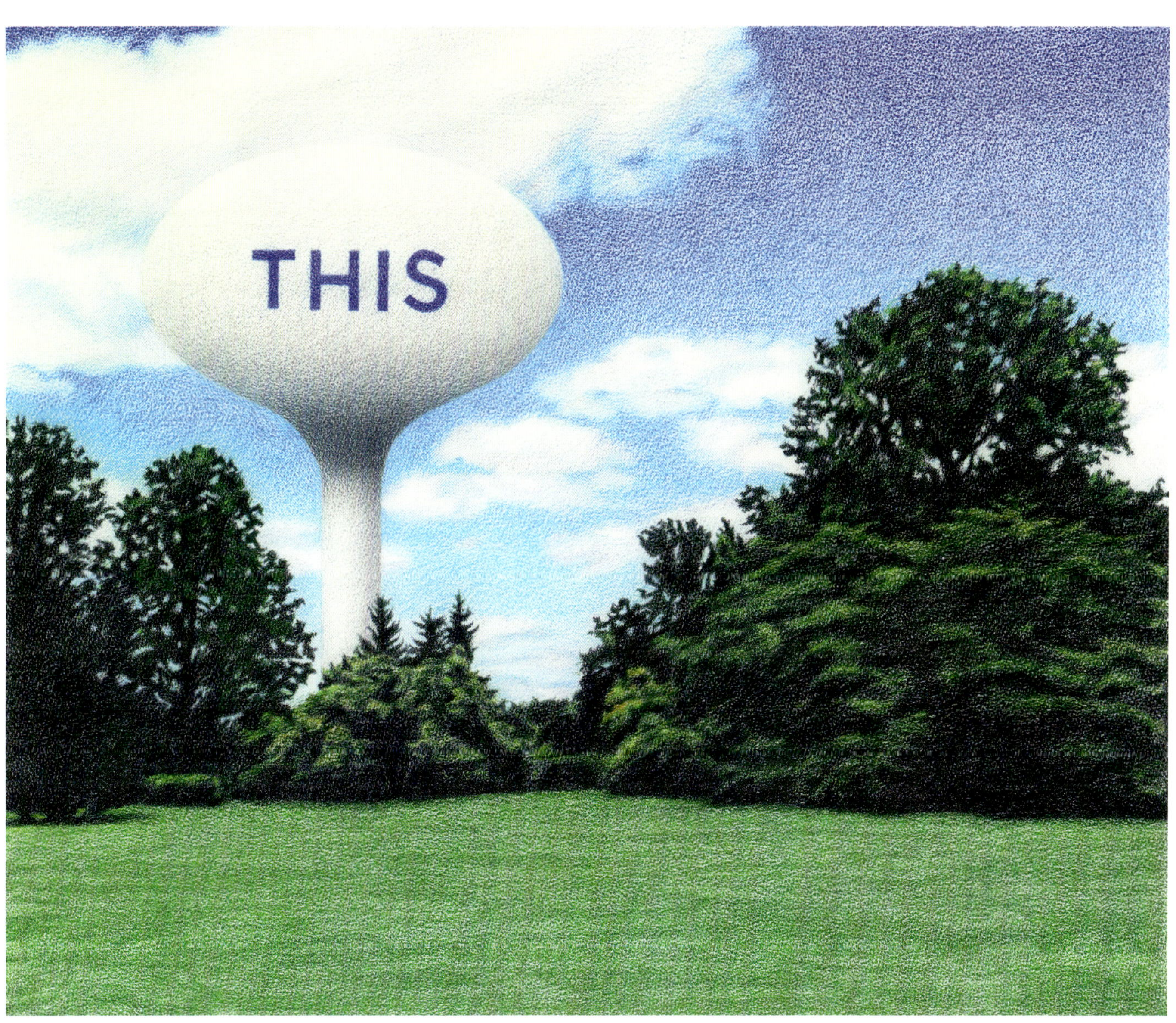
THIS

Yellow Pages, 2016
Colored pencil on paper
10⅛ × 18¾ inches

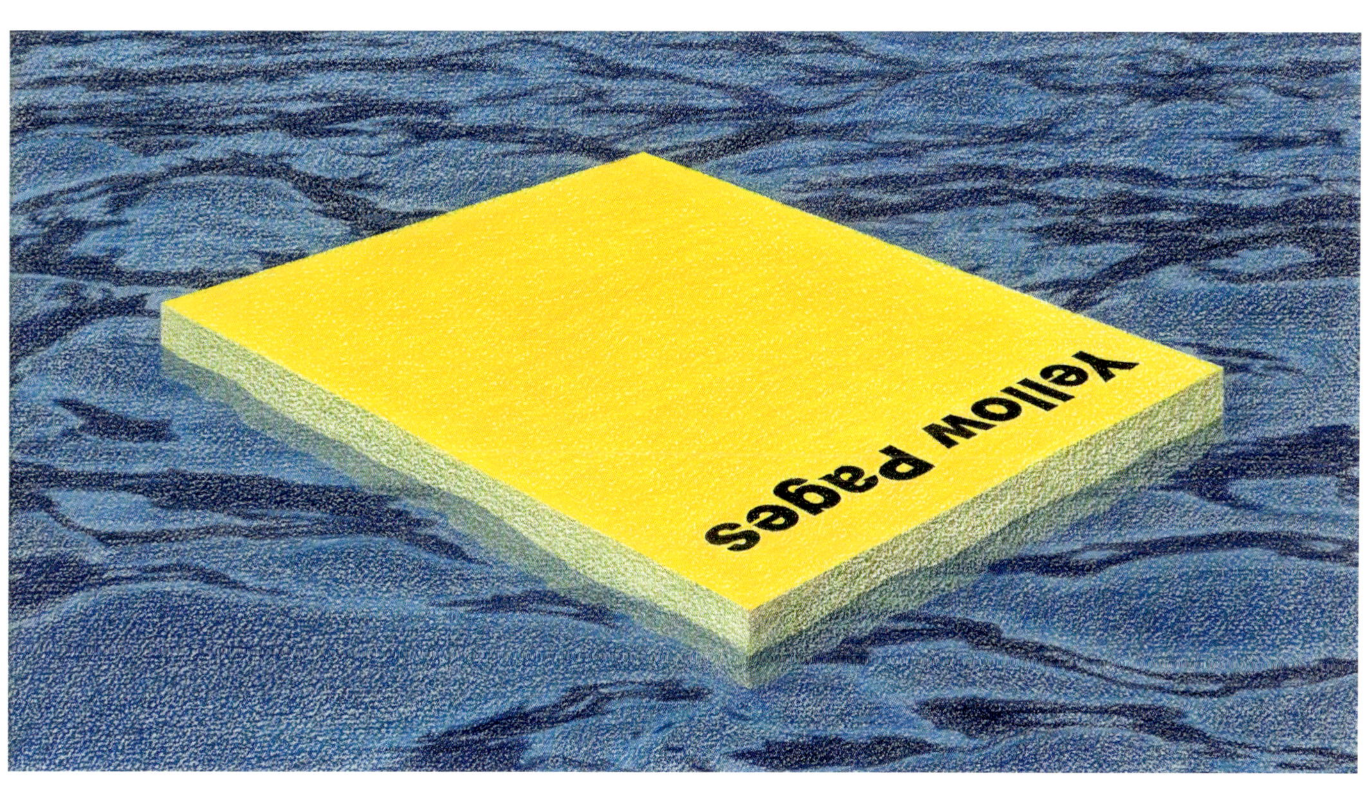
Yellow Pages

First Date, 2017
Colored pencil on paper
15 × 33 inches

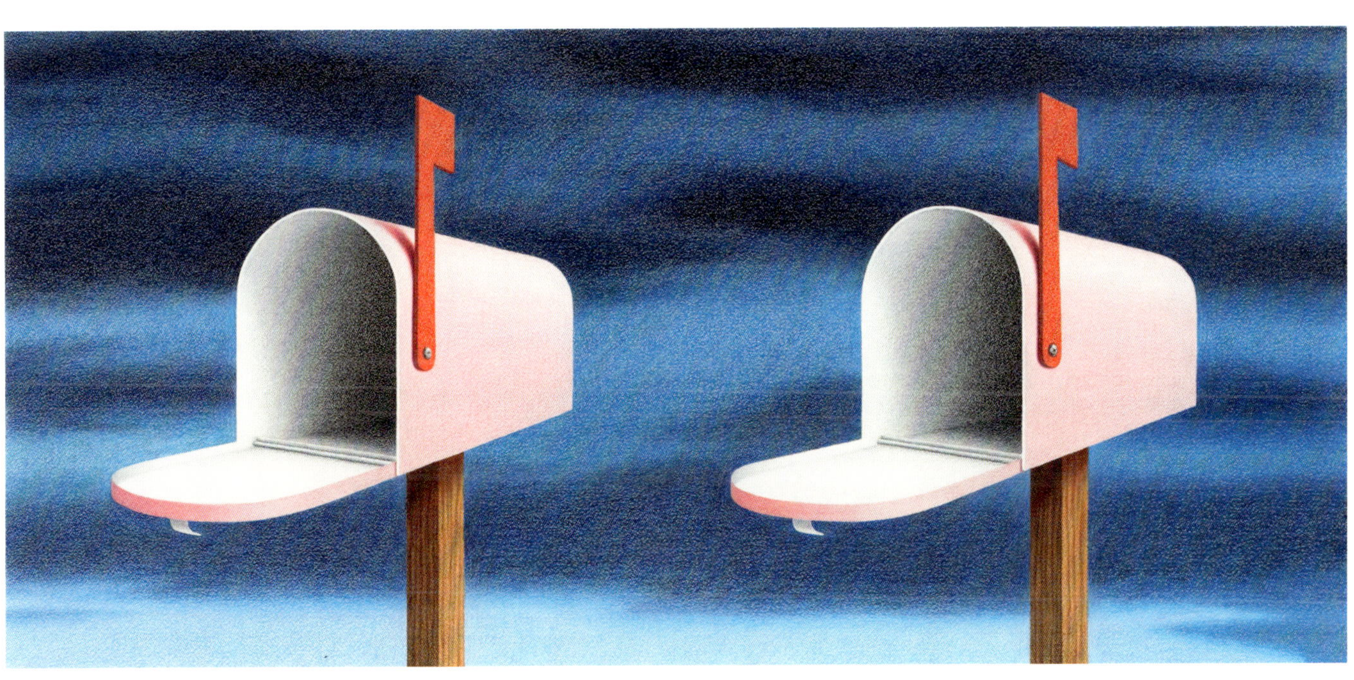

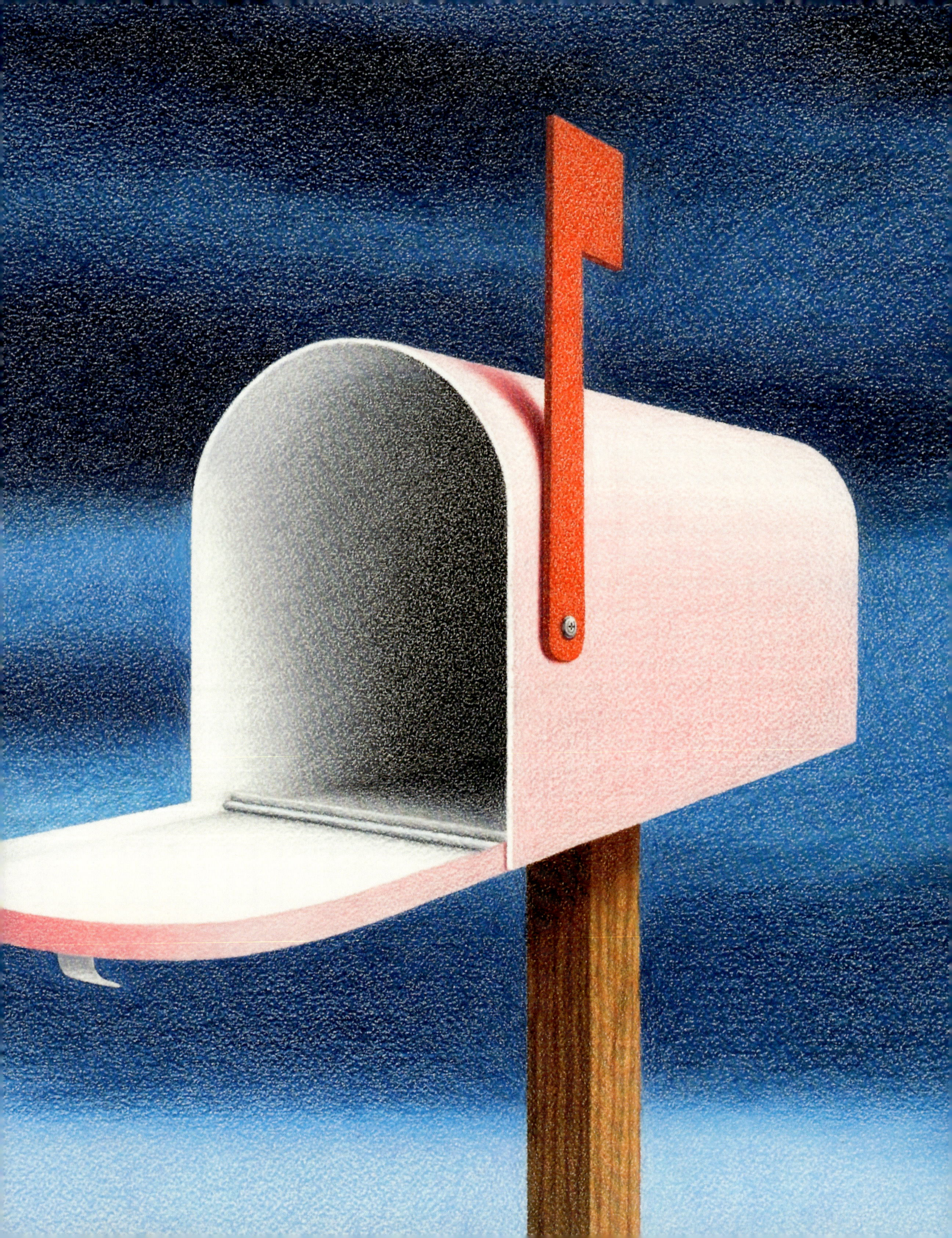

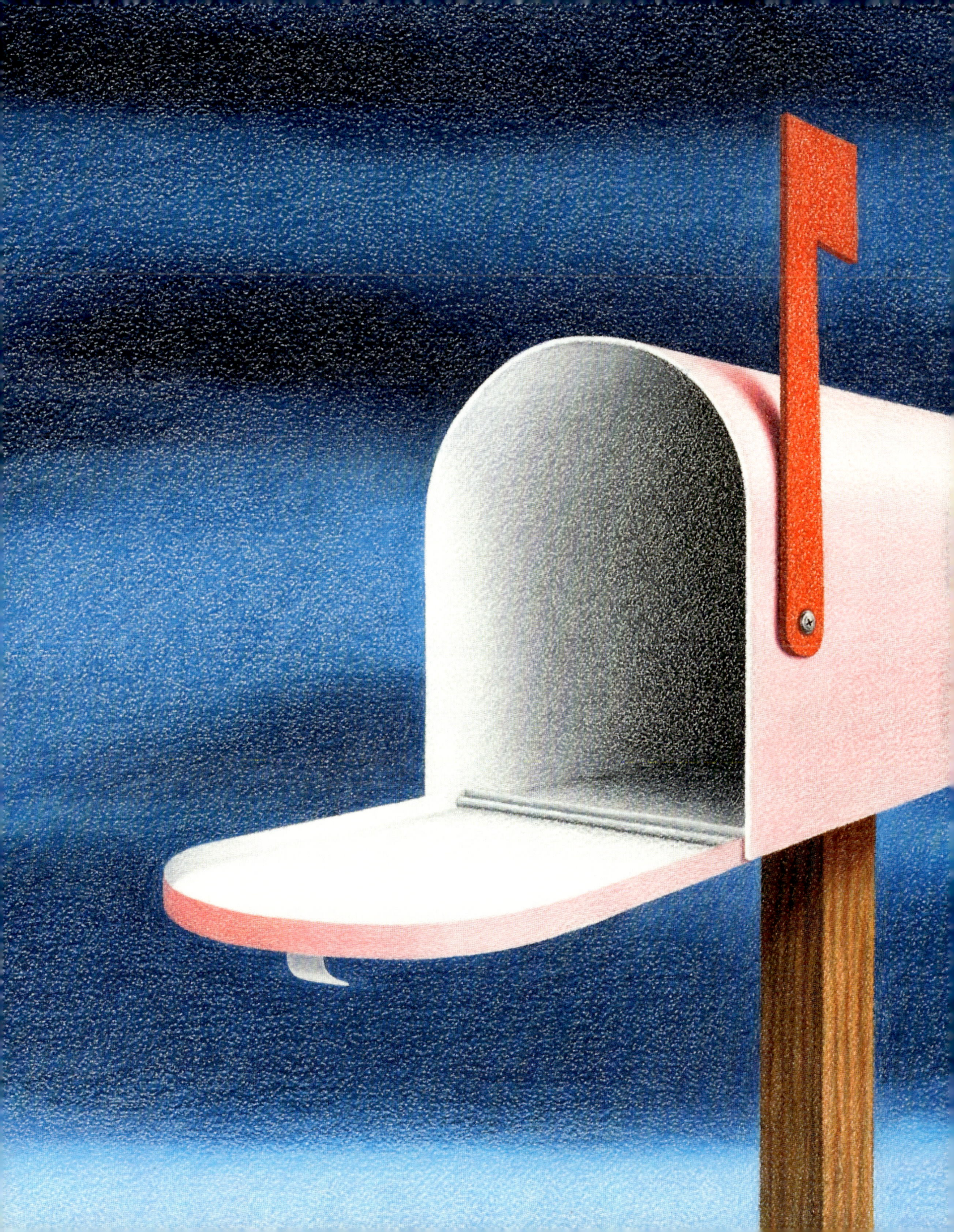

Lil Breezy, 2017
Colored pencil on paper
13½ × 19½ inches

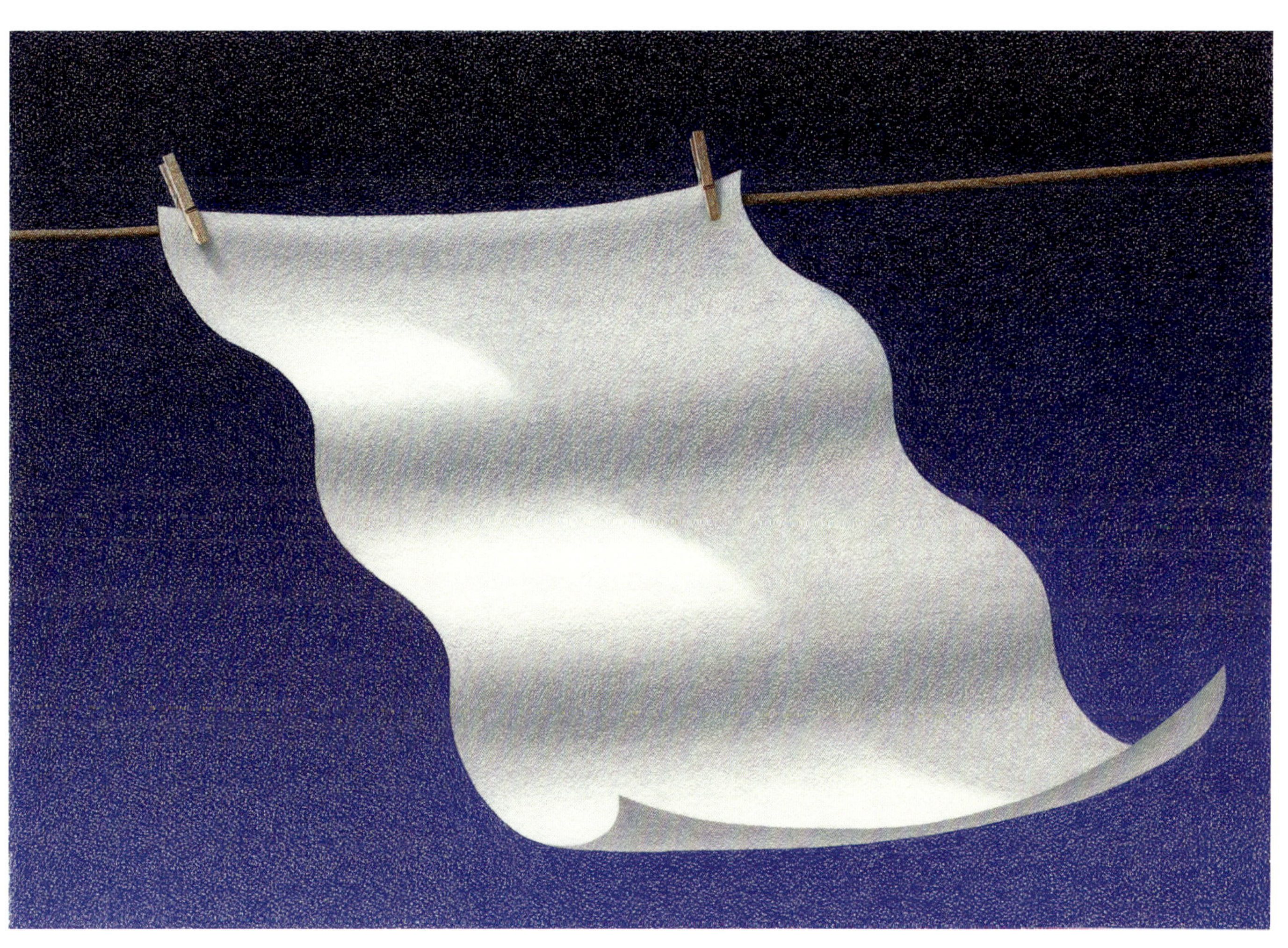

Rommely Rommel, 2017
Colored pencil on paper
18 × 14 inches

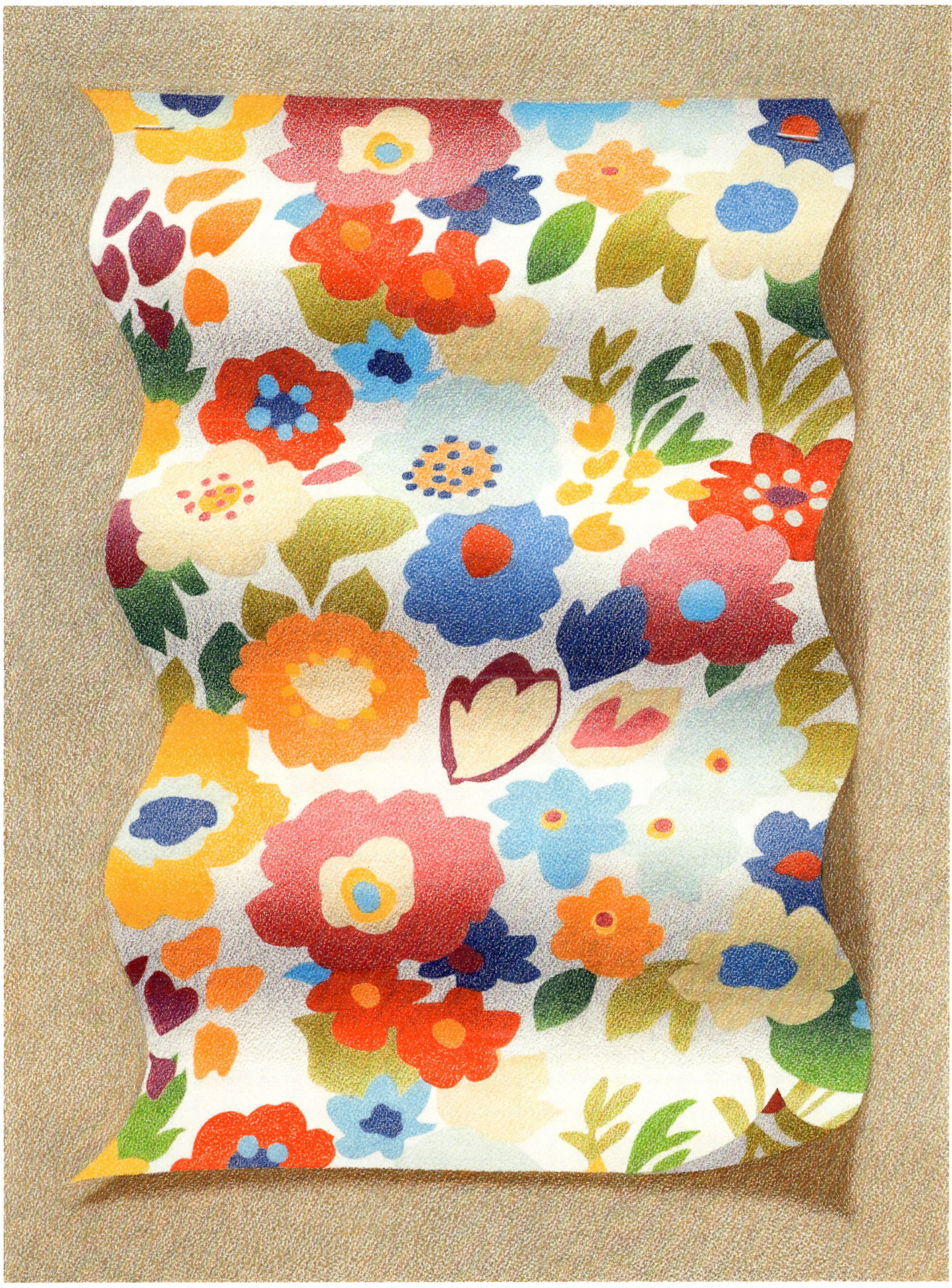

Garden, 2021
Colored pencil on paper
24 × 25 inches

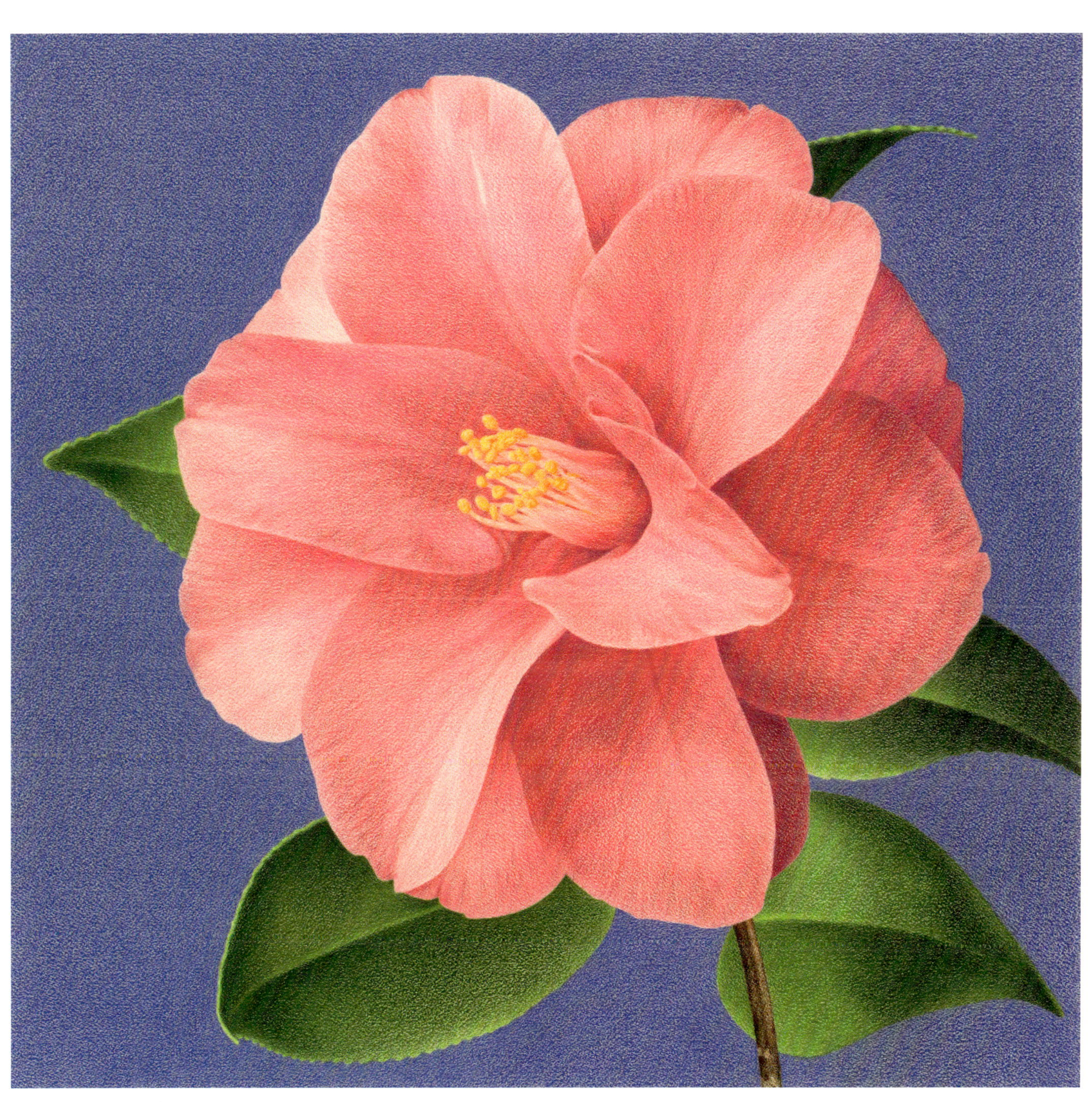

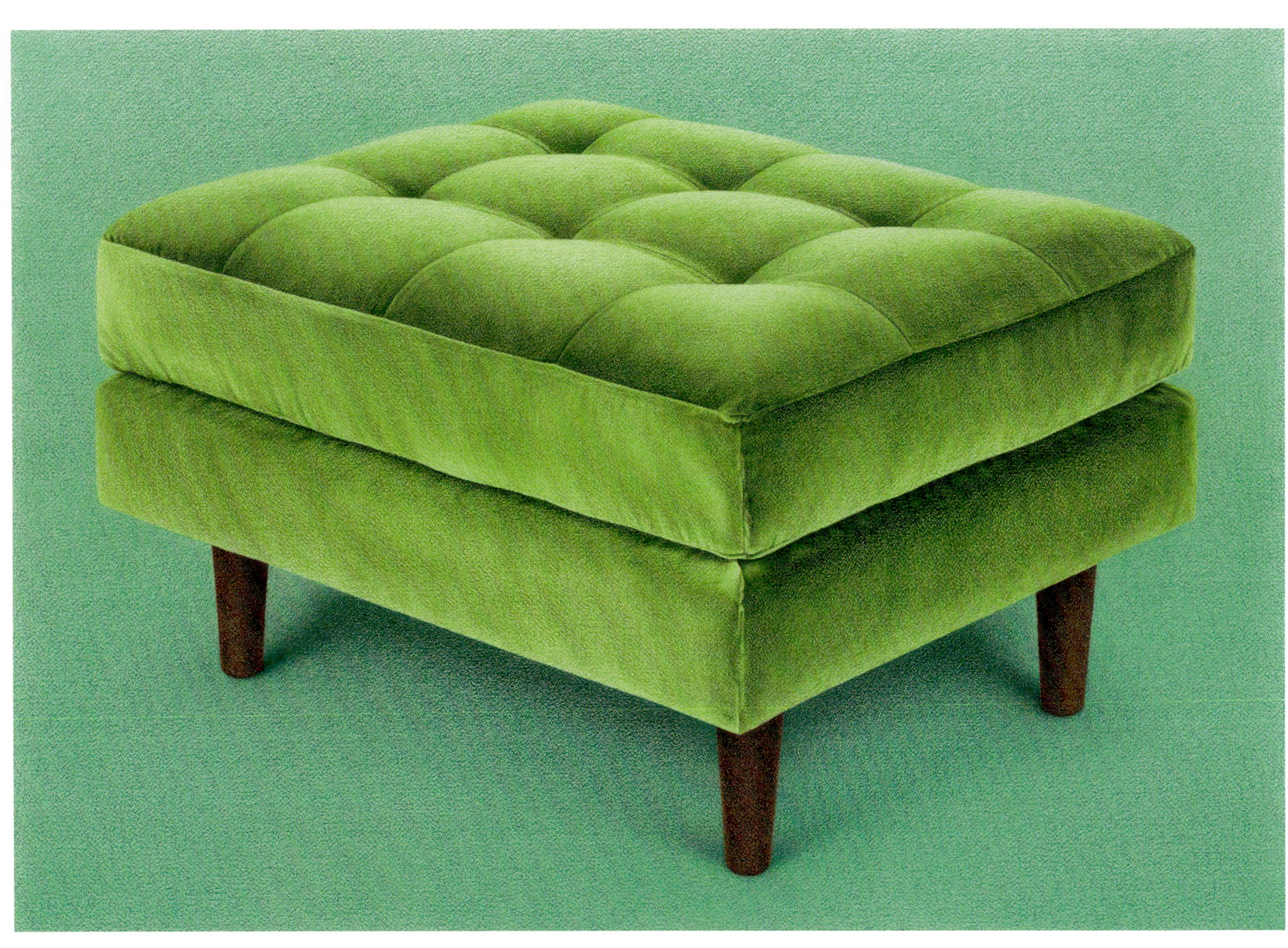

Ottoman, 2021
Colored pencil on paper
22 × 32 inches

Hand in Bed, 2016
Colored pencil on paper
17½ × 13 inches

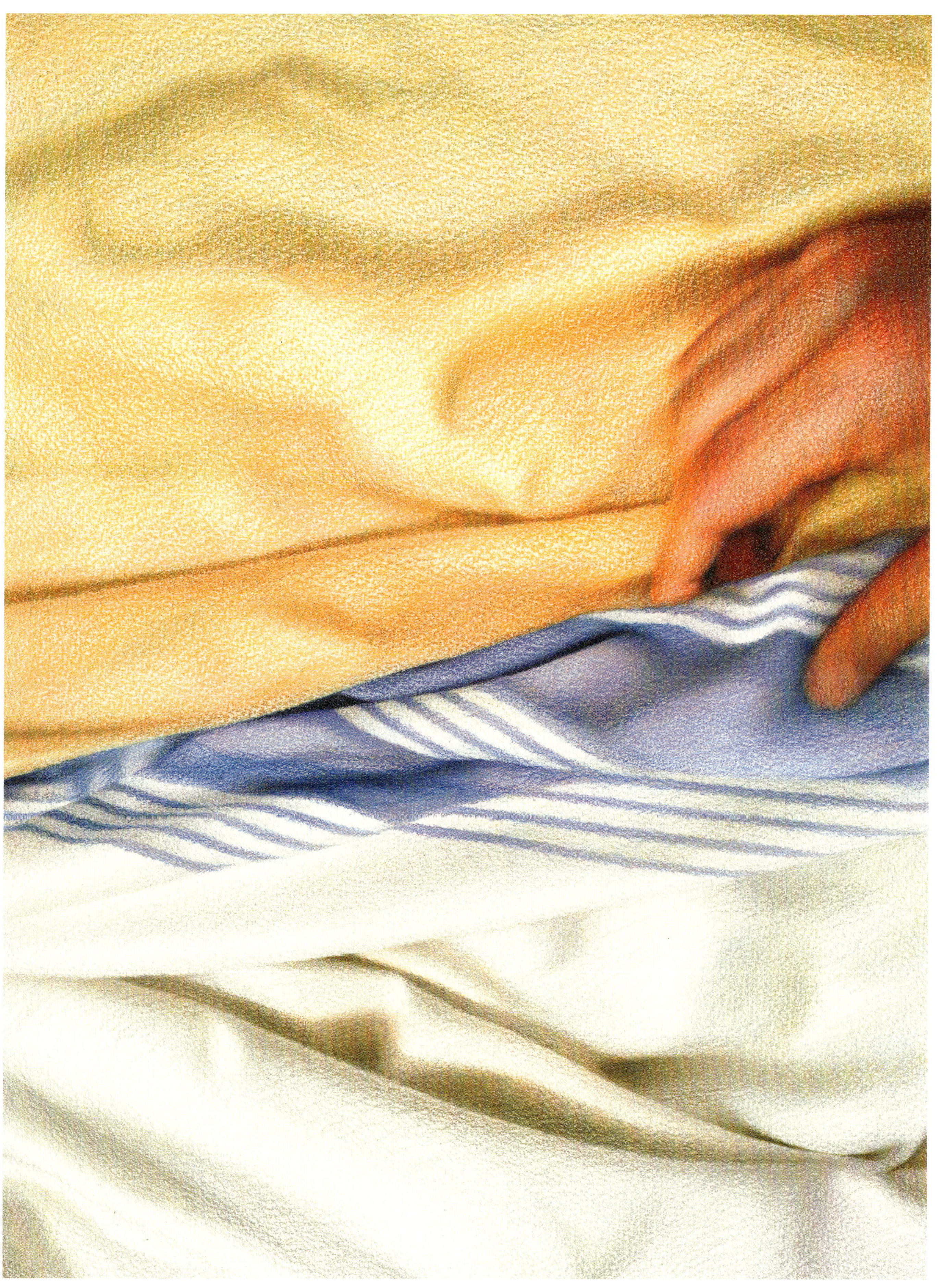

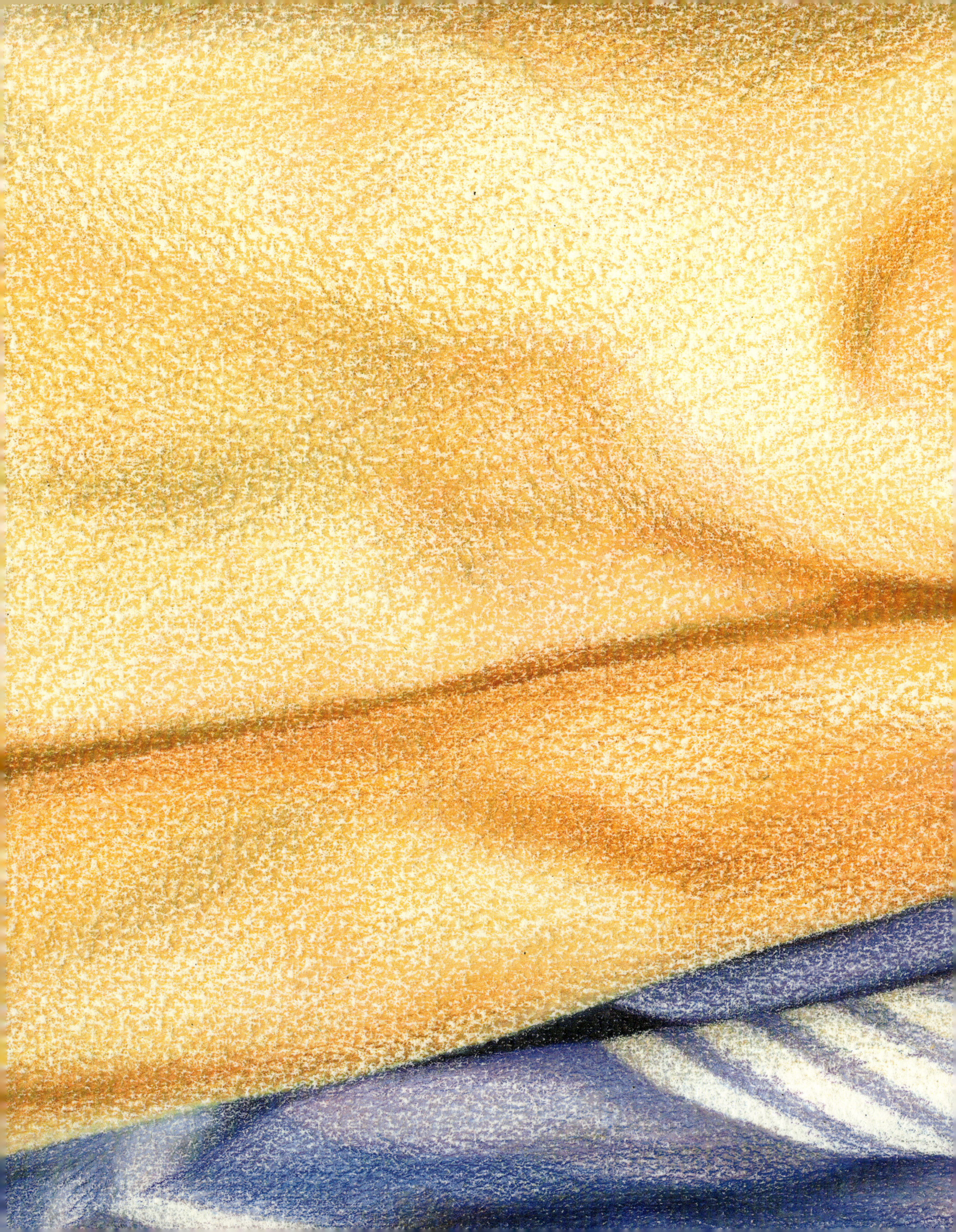

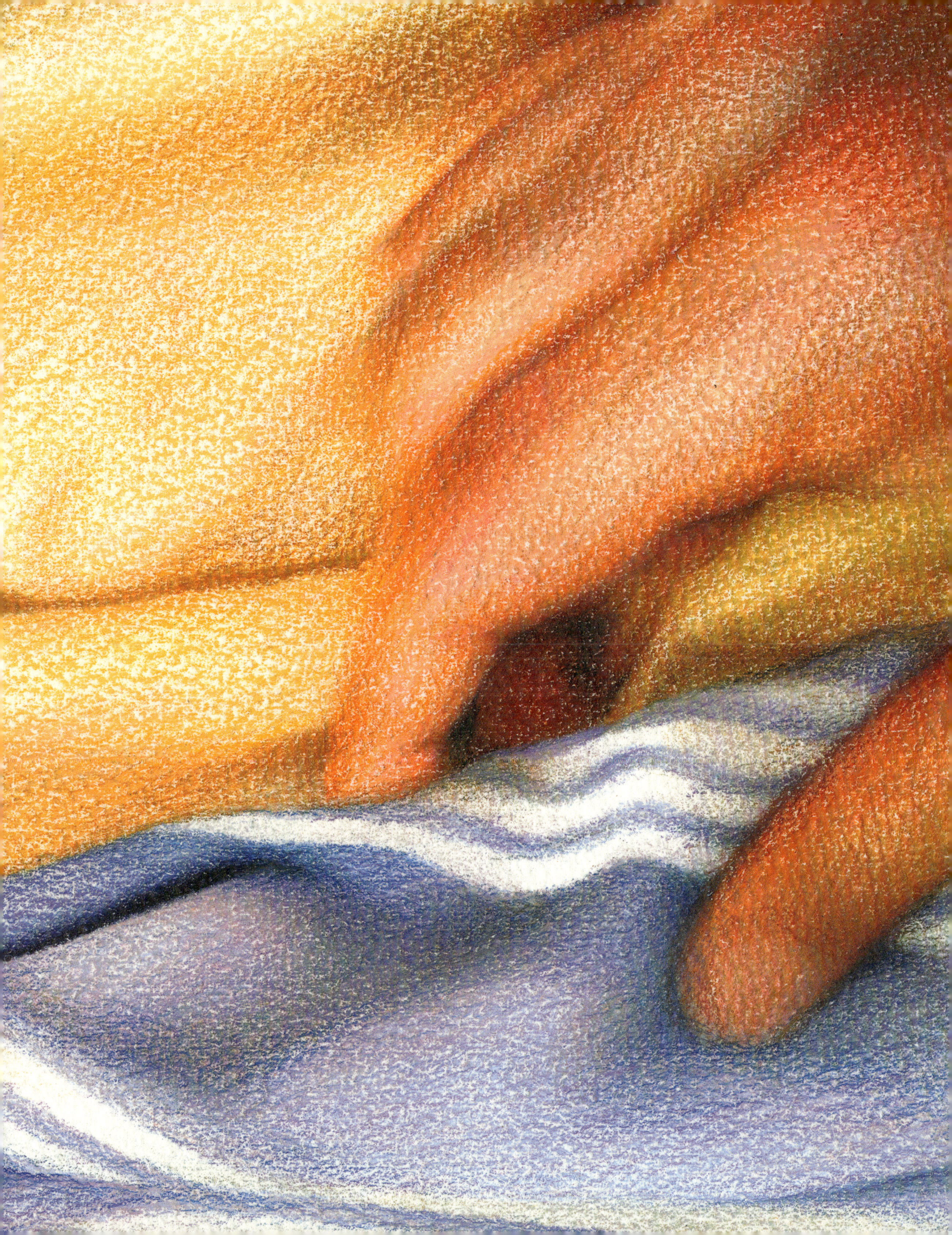

Flower Pot, 2020
Colored pencil on paper
25⅝ × 24½ inches

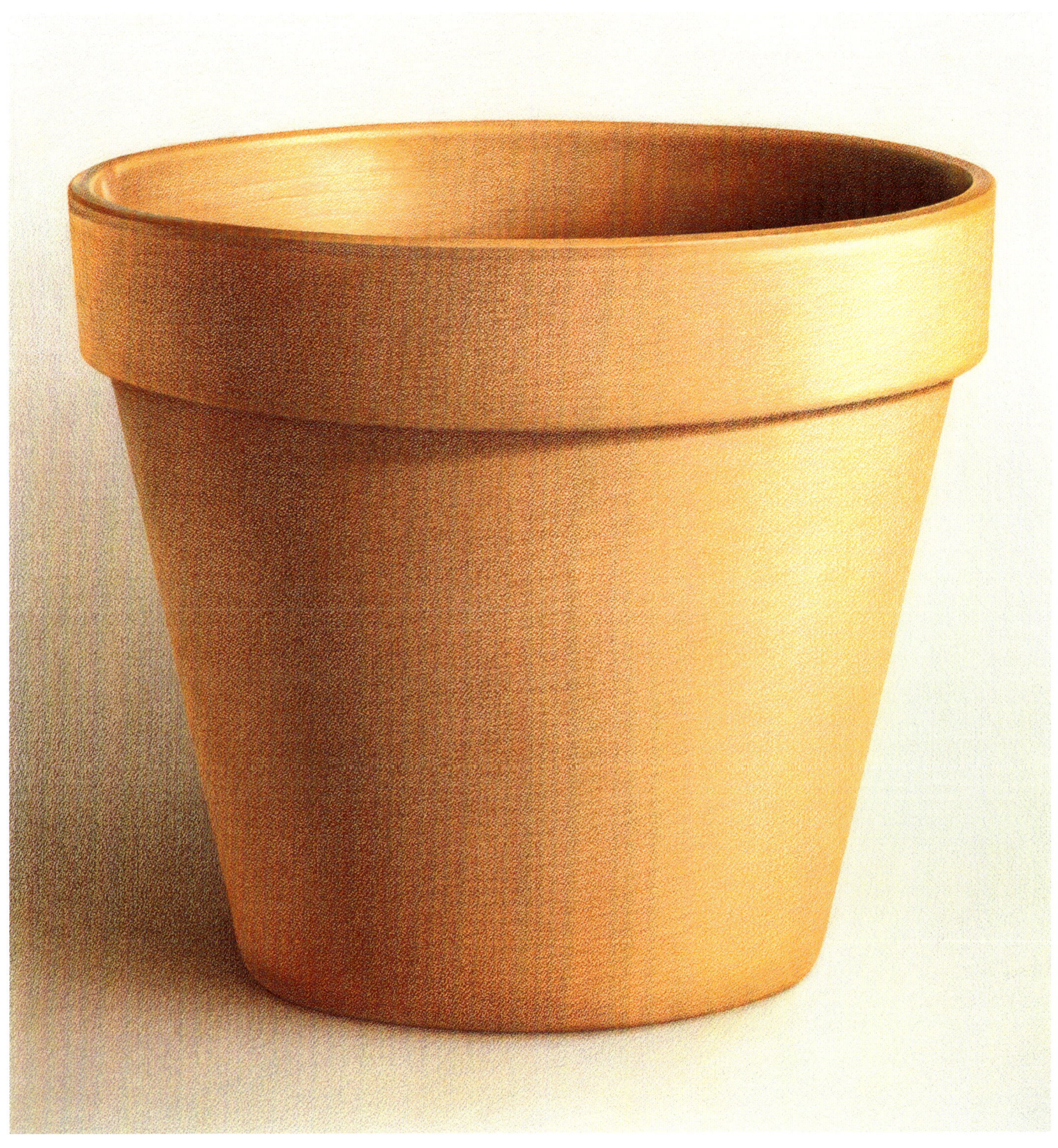

Pink Tiger, 2018
Colored pencil on paper
30 × 30 inches

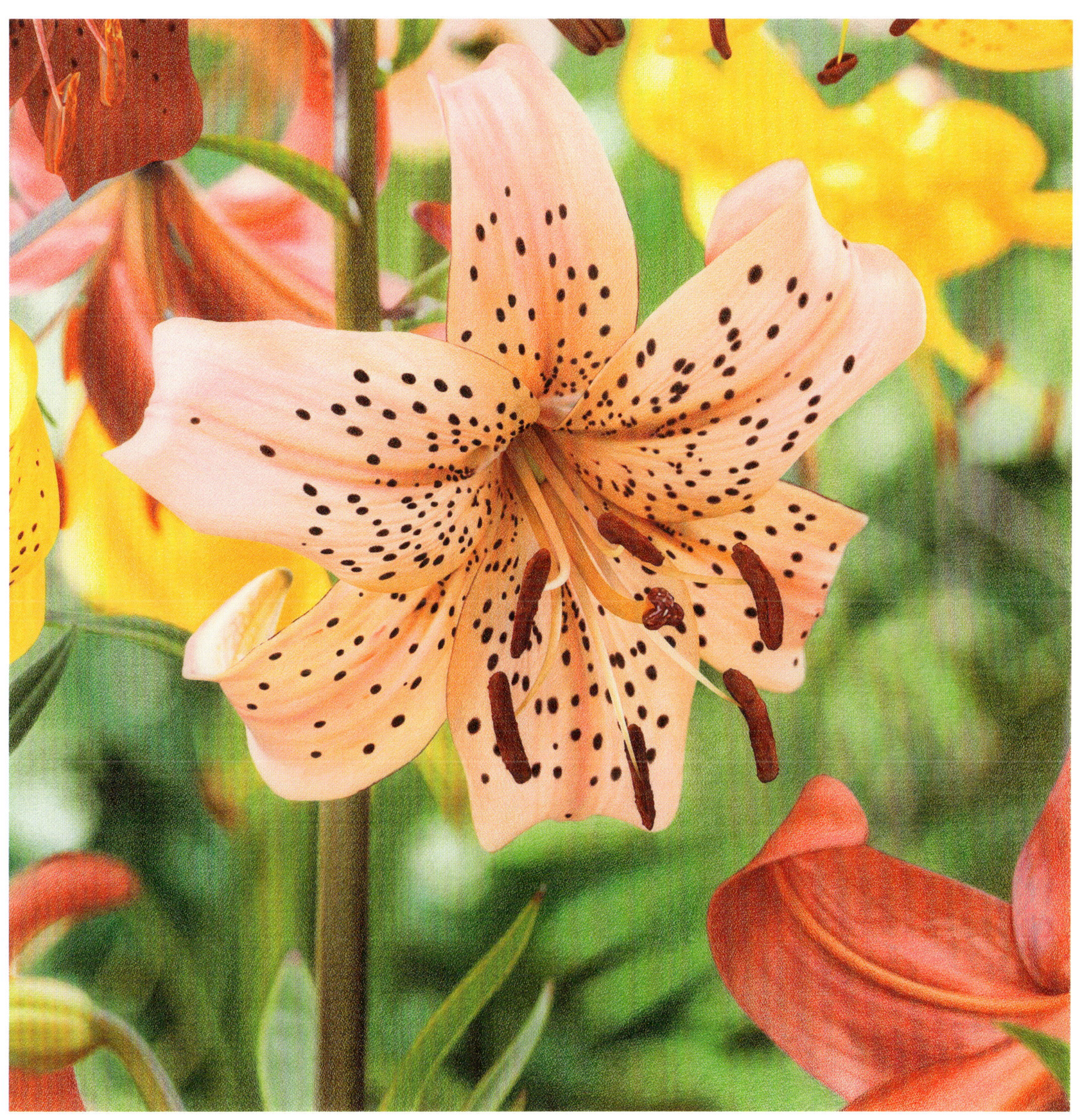

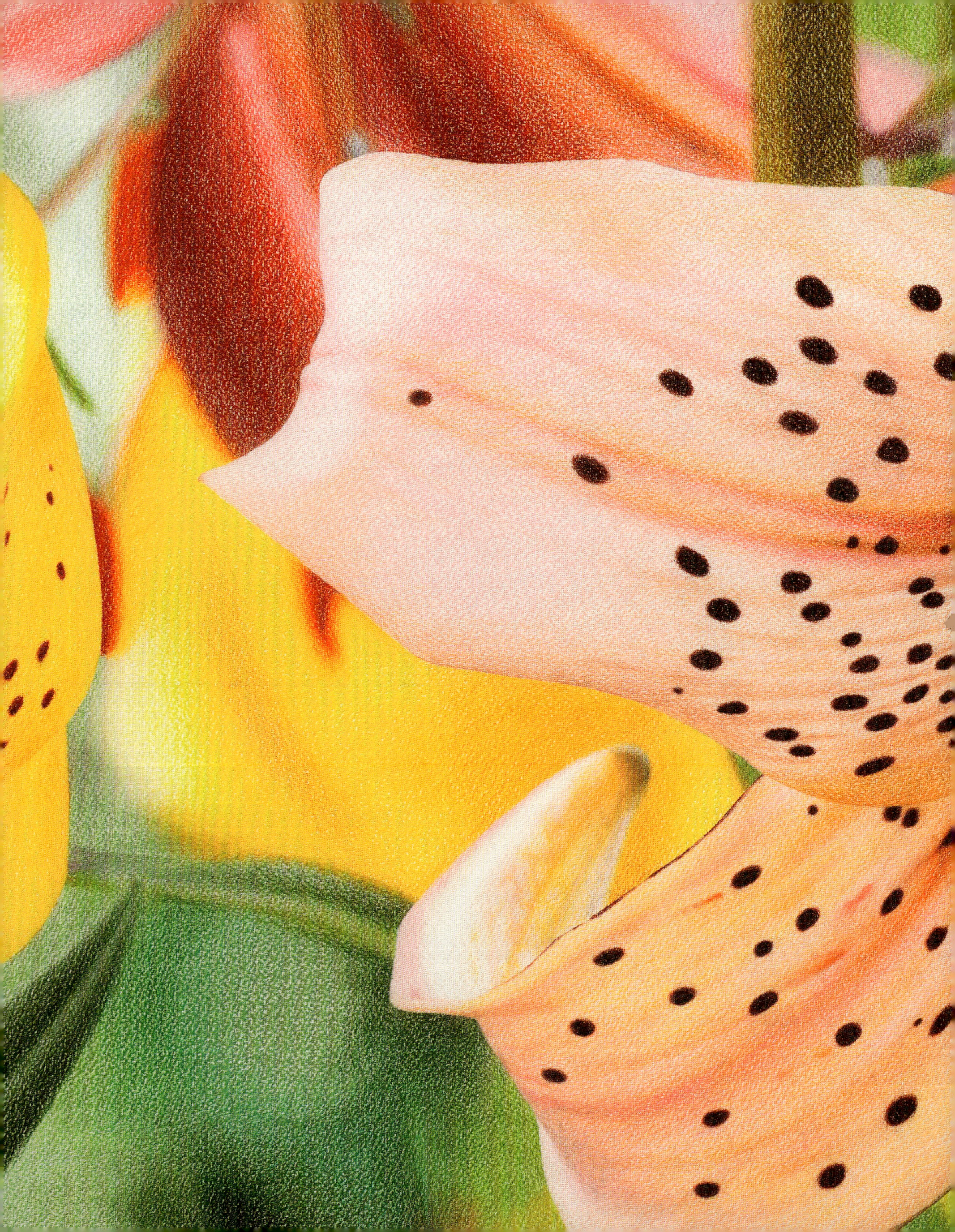

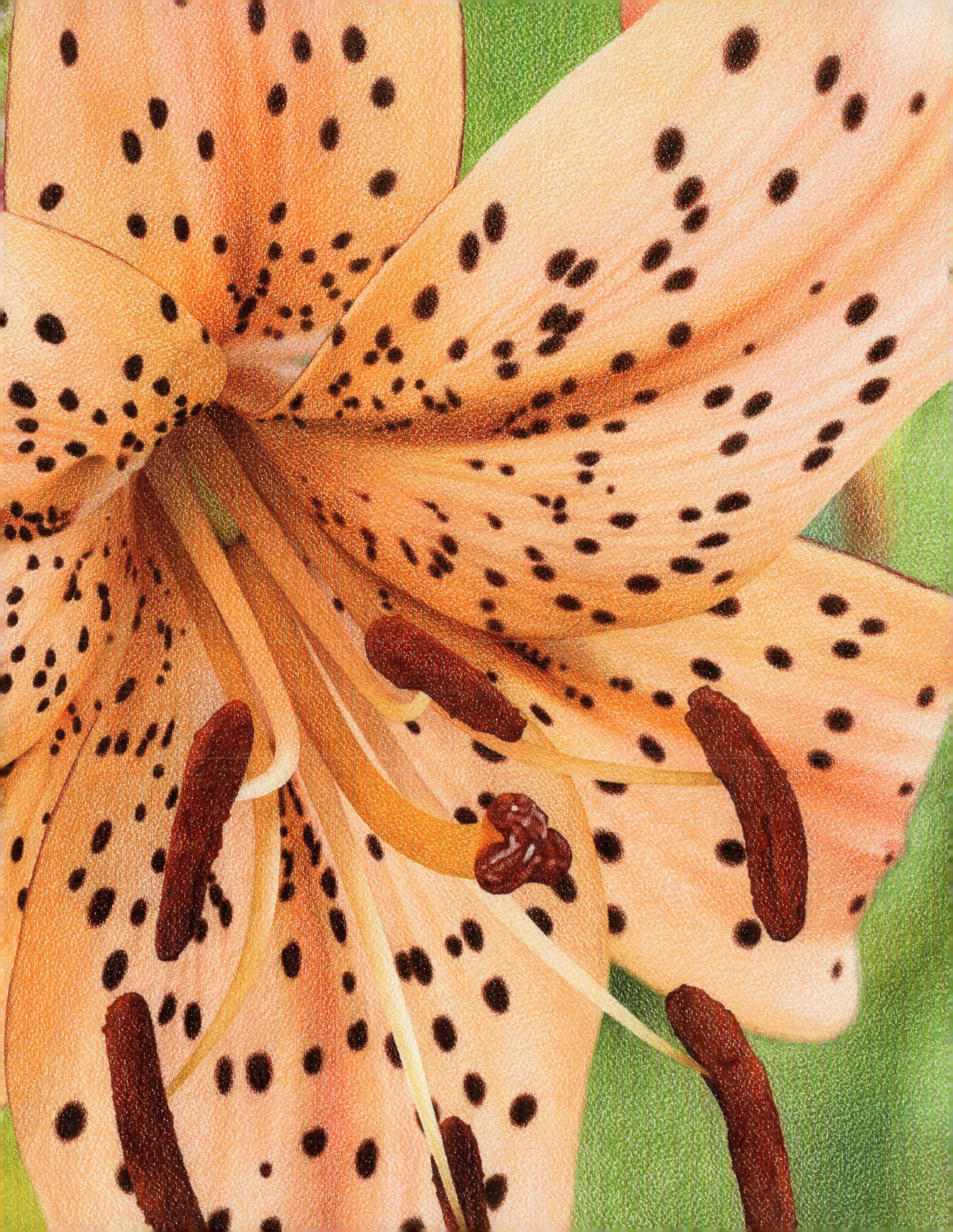

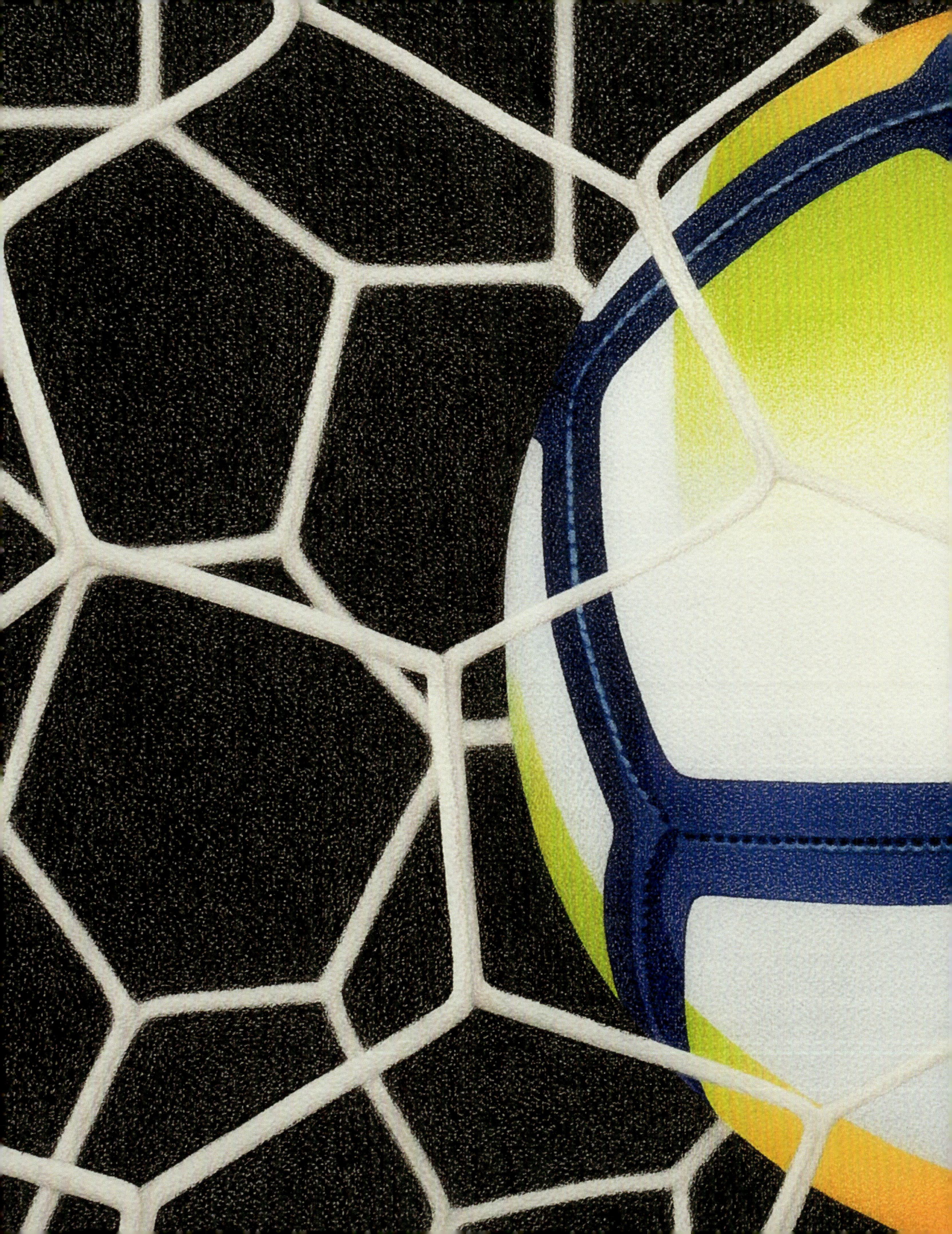

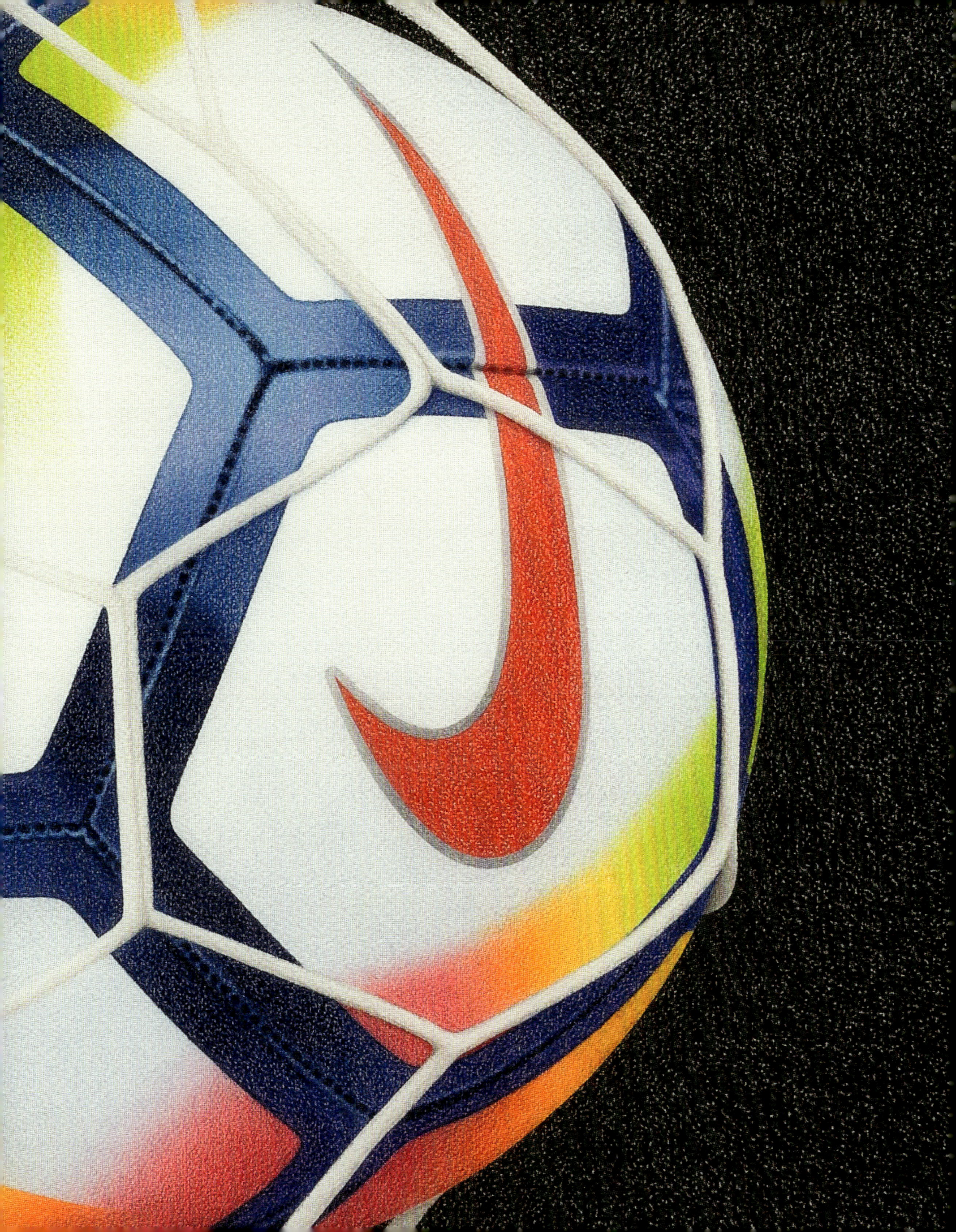

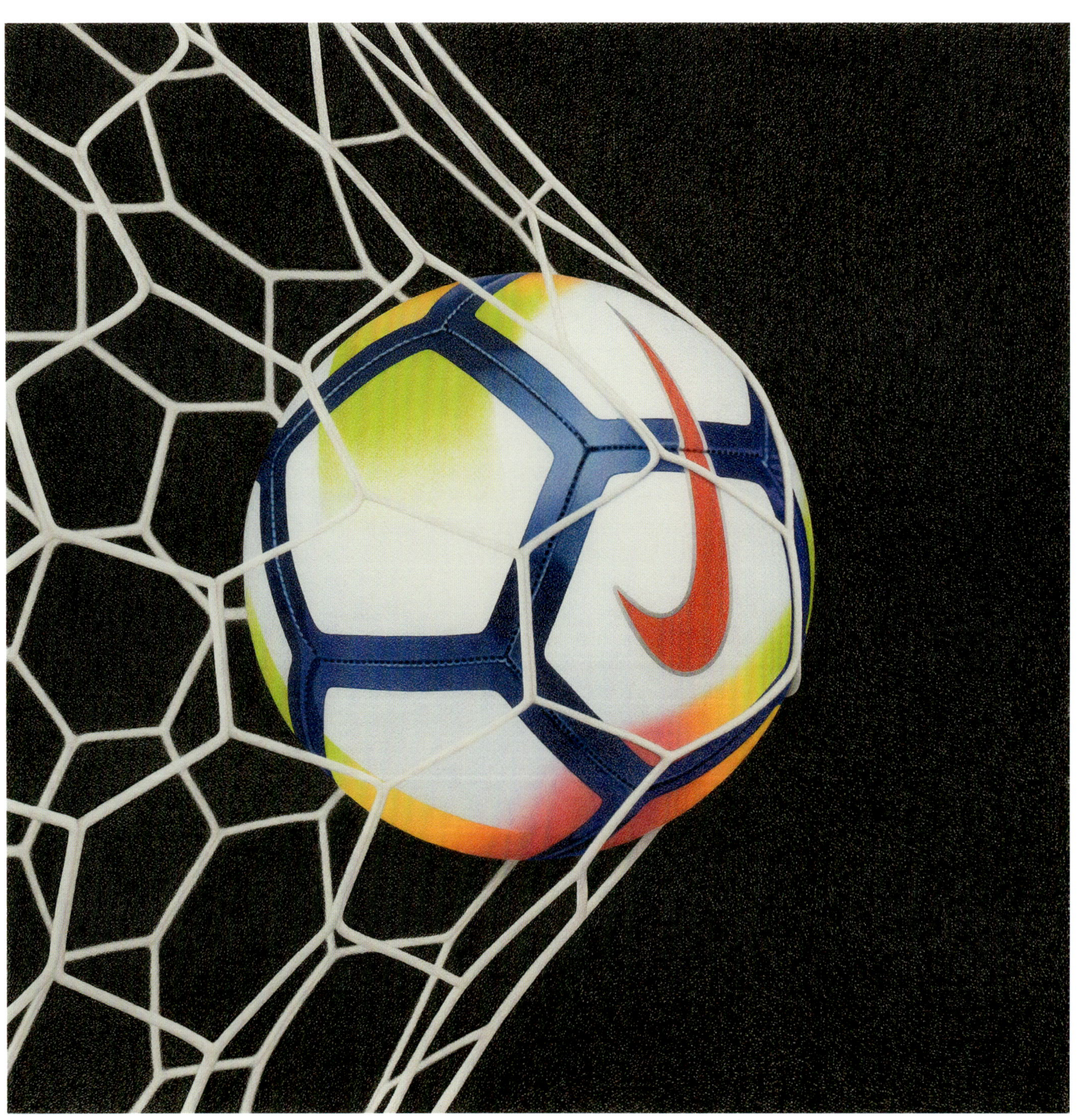

Stoppage Time, 2018
Colored pencil on paper
24 × 24 inches

Keeper, 2018
Colored pencil on paper
25½ × 25½ inches

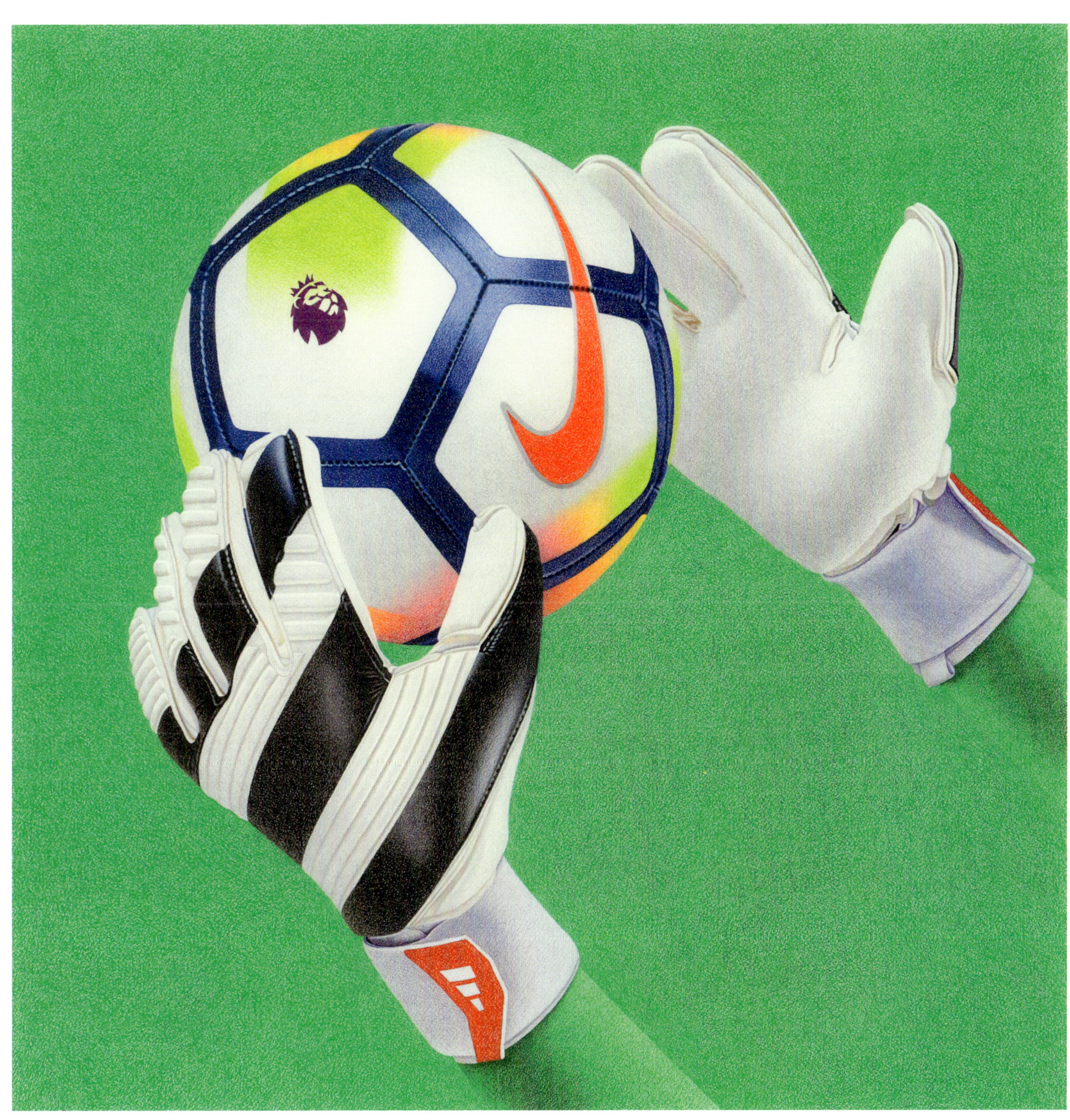

Kohler, 2007
Graphite on paper
12½ × 16¾ inches

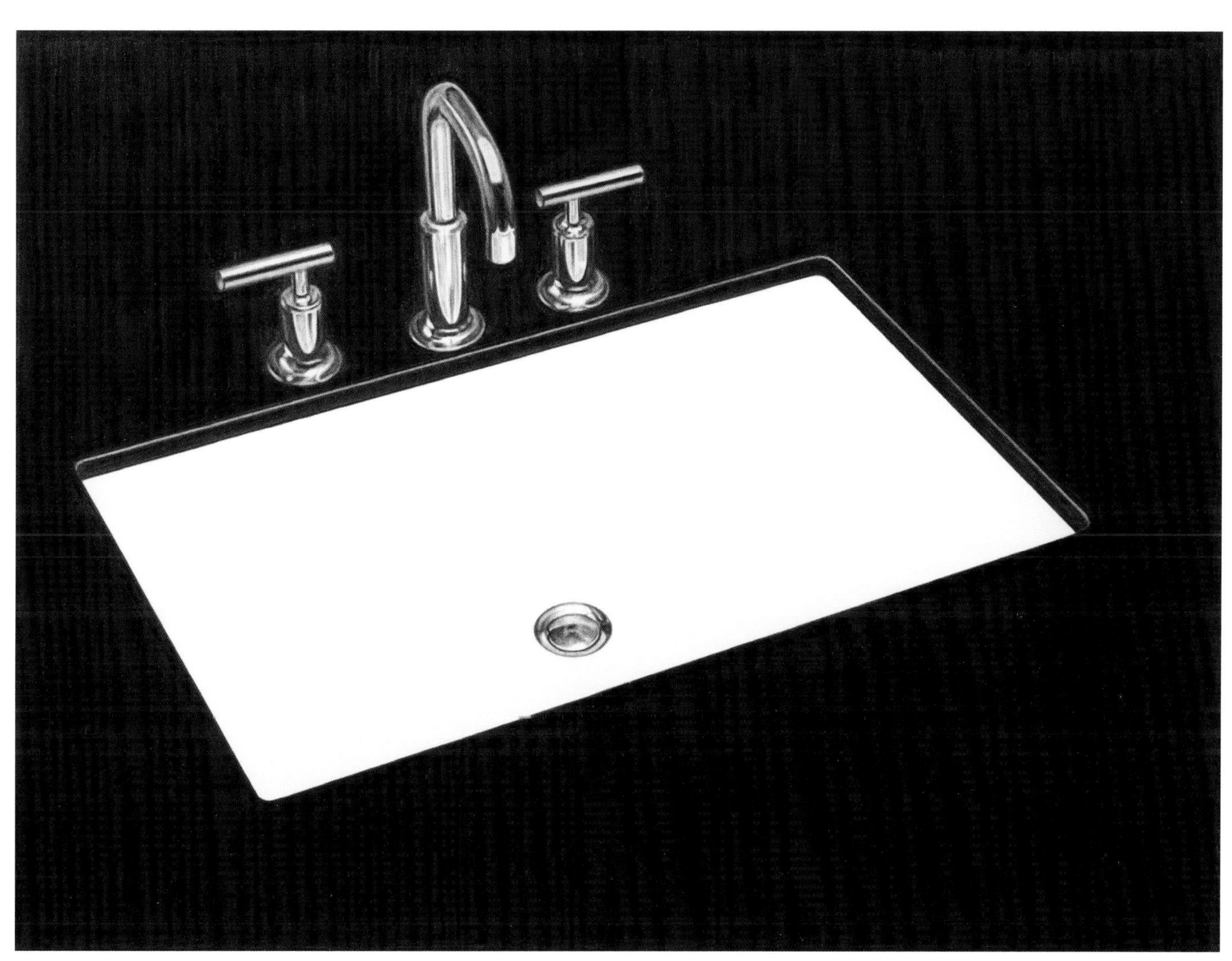

Sconce, 2021
Colored pencil on paper
23 × 25½ inches